Country Walks
in and around
Warwickshire

Country Walks
in and around
Warwickshire

Ron Weston

© Ron Weston, 2011

Published by Sigma Leisure – an imprint of
Sigma Press, Stobart House, Pontyclerc, Penybanc Road
Ammanford, Carmarthenshire SA18 3HP

British Library Cataloguing in Publication Data

A CIP record for this book is available from the British Library

ISBN: 978-1-85058-870-2

Typesetting and Design by: Sigma Press, Ammanford, Carms

Maps: © Bute Cartographics

Photographs: © Ron Weston

Cover photographs:
main photograph: The Crooked Tower, Barcheston
below (left to right): Wootton Hall, Bradnocks Marsh, St Giles church at Chesterton, Farnborough Hall

Printed by: Bertforts Group Ltd, Stevenage

Disclaimer: The information in this book is given in good faith and is believed to be correct at the time of publication. Care should always be taken when walking in hill country. Where appropriate, attention has been drawn to matters of safety. The author and publisher cannot take responsibility for any accidents or injury incurred whilst following these walks. Only you can judge your own fitness, competence and experience. Do not rely solely on sketch maps for navigation: we strongly recommend the use of appropriate Ordnance Survey (or equivalent) maps.

Foreword

Hello and welcome to a book of circular walks, the longest being 5½ miles (9km) and all within a radius of 25 miles (40km) from Coventry, with advice on where to park.

Many of you will have followed my weekly Country Walks column in the *Coventry Telegraph* and this collection is perhaps a sum of my experiences.

Warwickshire is a fine county for walking with a variety of countryside, sometimes hilly and sometimes flat, but never too demanding and only one hours' drive from the glorious North Cotswolds.

This selection of walks takes you on a journey of picturesque villages and historic churches, stately homes and castles, famous gardens and medieval tracks bound together by a superb network of public footpaths and canal towpaths and occasionally spilling over into adjoining counties.

In Warwickshire, we have an excellent Countryside Recreation Team who strive to keep our footpaths open and walkable and you will encounter many new kissing gates replacing worn out stiles as well as countless new footbridges.

You will meet long distance footpaths such as the Centenary Way, The Heart of England Way, Coventry Way or the Arden Way and these are generally in the care of volunteers in cooperation with the County Council. In fact, we are indebted to an army of volunteers who assist the County Council in its footpath work and, on behalf of every walker, I say thank you.

The Ramblers Association is an organisation of volunteers who exist to promote and protect the footpath network on a national basis and its many local groups organise short and longer works for people of every ability, as well as much maintenance work. There are groups in Coventry, Southam, Rugby and Stratford who welcome new members.

Contact numbers can be obtained from your library or at central office, telephone 020 7339 8500.

I leave you in the certain knowledge that somewhere in this book you will find your favourite walk and hopefully our paths may cross along the way.

Happy Walking

Ron Weston
June 2011

Contents

Dedicated to Mr. V. Menon and his expert team at Coventry University Hospital, who delivered me through a successful stomach cancer operation, also to my wife Isobel and daughter Charlotte Kim for their after care.

If you meet animals

Give them a wide berth where possible.

Do not make eye contact.

Do not approach if they have young.

Do not run.

Release your dog from the lead if approached by cattle.

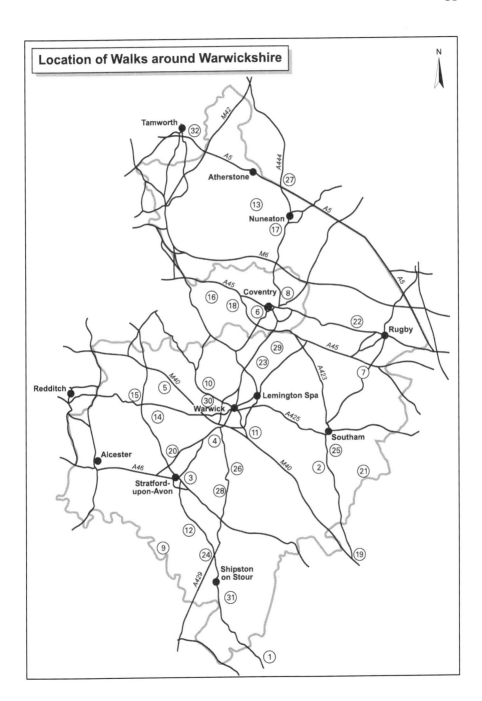

Walk 1: Long Compton –
Whichford Wood

Prepare for a few hills on this scenic walk. Long Compton sits at the bottom of two hills and on the return over Redliff Hill these words by Norman Gale are very apt.

> *We came at last upon the hills that keep,*
> *As mothers watch their babes asleep,*
> *Long Compton guarded in the vale;*
> *There as a dreaming child it lay*
> *And took the evening light.*

Distance: 4½ miles (7.25km)
Allow: 2¼ hours
Map: Ordnance Survey 1:25000 Explorer 191
Grid reference: 286328

How to get there:
From Coventry, follow the A423 to Princethorpe and turn right onto the Fosse Way. Continue through Halford and turn left at the next island to Shipston on the A3400. Bear right after the church still on the A3400 and go on to Long Compton. Turn right after the church at the Barton sign and park on the left.

The Route:
Walk back towards Shipston and a minor road to Whichford which forks right. Turn right at the waymarked garden fence to follow a short track into a field and go straight ahead past a pond on your right to join a cart road. Follow it upward into a field and go on, with the wood on the left, into the corner. Enter the wood and follow the track to the top of the hill and turn right to exit at a large field on your right and the wood on the left. Walk on for a quarter mile (400m) to a short waymark post on the left, which you will return to.

Continue along the edge of the wood and pass another waymark post on the end of a hedge coming in from the right. Follow the edge of

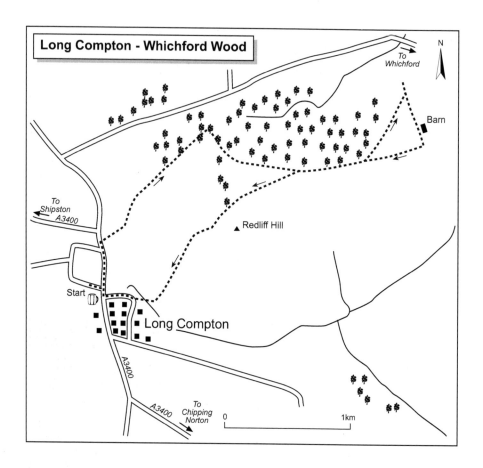

the wood as it veers to the left and enters the trail through the trees to exit into a large field. With the wood on the left, go to the bottom corner of the field but do not turn right. Enter the trail into the wood and descend through the bracken to exit into a field with the village of Whichford ahead. Go forward to a hedge corner at the edge of the village but we do not enter the village. Turn about to climb the hill to some old fencing with a waymark, when it comes into view. Go up the steep bank on the left side of the waymark and bear right to reach a stile at the top of the hill. Walk straight ahead to pass the barns on your left and at the hedge line turn right on this side of the hedge and maintain direction over an open field to rejoin the edge of the wood.

Retrace your steps to the waymark post you located earlier and veer left across the open field until you reach a green farm track across your path. At this point you should be midway between the wood on your right and a hedge corner on your left. Continue ahead to enter the wood at a waymark post and descend the trail to exit over a stile into a field. Descend along the foot of the hill using the waymark posts and climb a stile into the next field and follow the hedge on the left to a stile in the corner and step onto a farm track. Cross the open field bearing right to reach a footbridge and stay in the same direction to exit onto a lane and then turn right to the main road. Turn right to return to the church.

Near Long Compton

Walk 2: Priors Hardwick – Oxford Canal

Priors Hardwick was gifted to the monks of Coventry by Earl Leofric, hence its name. Close by is the ancient Welsh Road where the drovers moved their cattle and geese to the markets in the south. This brought prosperity to the village and the weather vane on the church tower depicts a drover in traditional smock.

A pleasant walk with stunning views at the start and a good canal towpath.

Distance:	4 miles (6.5km)
Allow:	2 hours
Map:	Ordnance Survey 1:25000 Explorer 206
Grid reference:	471561

How to get there:
From Coventry, follow the A423 onto the Southam bypass and turn left onto the Daventry Road A425 and immediately turn right at the Priors Hardwick sign. Continue for four miles (6.5km) and after the canal bridge turn right and right again to the centre of the village. Park in the vicinity of the church and the Butchers Arms.

The Route:
The walk begins up the steps in the centre of the Butchers Arms car park. Climb the stile and turn right to cross a pair of in-line stiles to enter a private garden and go ahead to exit onto the lane. Cross to the kissing gate opposite and turn diagonally right to the left side of the house and go on to a gate in the field corner. Follow the field edge along the top of the ridge into the second field and veer right down the hill, staying close to the small wood on the left. Aim for the yellow post and kissing gate in the dry ditch and maintain direction in the next field to exit onto the road.

Cross to the gate opposite and continue diagonally left up the middle of the field to reach the drive of Stoneton Manor. Walk on for 50 yards (46m) and turn right down the track to the farm buildings. Go forward

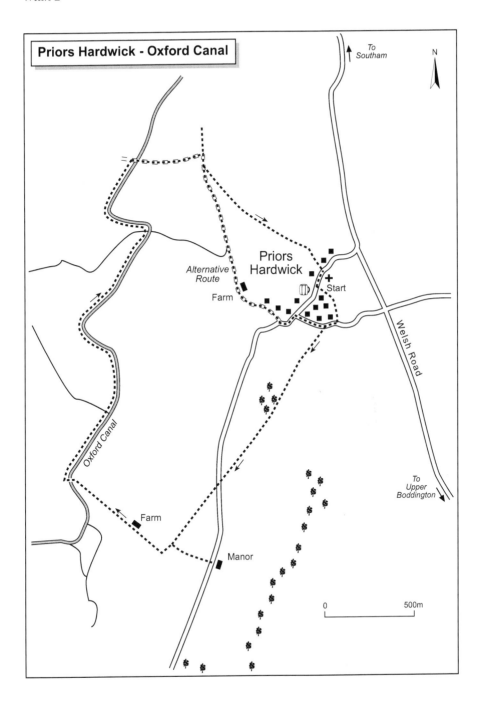

Priors Hardwick - Oxford Canal

The Butchers Arms - Priors Hardwick

in the field on the right side of the buildings to join the canal towpath at bridge No. 126 and follow the water on your right to bridge No. 123. Turn right over the bridge and follow the farm track until it turns sharp right with a waymarked gate on the left. Turn right with the track to reach a gate across your path in 150 yards (135m), where you have a choice of two routes.

Option 1: Remain on the track to reach a road junction and bear left and left again to return to the Butchers Arms.

Option 2: Bear diagonally left across the open field to the corner and stay in the same direction in the next field to the next corner. Climb the stile into a green path and go straight ahead to exit in front of the church.

Walk 3: Stratford and River Avon

On this walk you will come face to face with the recent urban sprawl of Stratford, which at the time caused concern for many townsfolk. Fortunately the footpaths have been retained almost intact and thousands of trees have been planted in a conservation area with display panels to describe the local flora and fauna. The River Avon and the Old Tramway form the rest of the walk which is suitable for every season.

Distance: 3½ miles (5.5km)
Allow: 1½ hours
Map: Ordnance Survey 1:25000 Explorer 205
Grid reference: 195540

How to get there:

Go to Stratford from Coventry via the A46 and A439 and turn left over the river bridge to an island. Turn right on the A3400 and at the next island turn right into Seven Meadows Road and follow it to the Greenway free car park on the left. Note the closing times on the gate.

The Route:

Cross the road with care into Old Town Mews and follow it to the end. Enter the tarmac path and cross a residential road to follow the path down to the river. Cross the footbridge and turn left on the river path to pass Holy Trinity and the Royal Shakespeare Theatre. Veer right to pass the bandstand on your left and go forward through the car park to the entrance to the Butterfly Farm. Turn right on to the Riverbank Walk, known as the Old Tramway, and follow it for a half mile (800m) to exit at a traffic island.

Turn left across the Shipston Road and cross Trinity Way to a waymarked kissing gate and descend through the centre of the wildlife meadow. Turn left beneath the road bridge and turn right over the footbridge to head up the centre of the field to the left corner. Turn left to join the road and turn right to Dryden Way on your right.

Holy Trinity church and the River Avon - Stratford

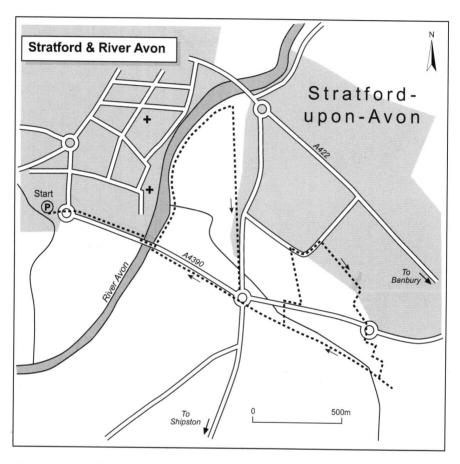

Turn right and continue past Bridgetown House to exit onto Betjeman Road and bear left to follow Wordsworth Avenue to an island on Trinity Way. Cross to a kissing gate on the right side of the farm road and follow the path around the angles to a display panel where the path divides and turn sharp right. Follow the hedge on the right to return to the road bridge and retrace your steps up the centre of the wildlife meadow to join the main road.

Cross to the enclosed path on the left side of Seven Meadows Road and follow it down to the river. Turn right beneath the bridge and turn left over the footbridge to retrace your steps back to Old Town Mews and the car park opposite.

Walk 4: Hockley Heath – Lapworth

It is believed the busy A3400 through Hockley Heath was a route laid down long before the Romans trod this path. It became a coaching road between Birmingham and the capital and brought prosperity to the village for inn keepers, wheelwrights and blacksmiths. With the coming of the canals, Hockley adapted to the new form of transport and the Wharf Tavern is a reminder of those early days where a host of materials were loaded or unloaded.

This would make a good winter walk.

Distance:	4 miles (6.5km)
Allow:	2 hours
Map:	Ordnance Survey 1:25000 Explorer 220
Grid reference:	153725

How to get there:
Follow the B4101 from Coventry through Knowle to Hockley Heath and turn left onto A3400. Turn left at the Warwick sign onto B4439 and park in the parish car park on the left. Note the closing times on the gate.

The Route:
Cross the main road to the Wharf Tavern and turn left and then right into Spring Lane. Turn left into Nuthurst Lane next to the church and follow it to the first lane on the left. Turn left up the hill and go on to reach the main road and cross carefully. Turn left and right into Wharf Lane and follow it to turn first right into Spring Lane. Continue past Spring Farm to Lapworth Farm, both on the left, and in a further 80 yards (73m) turn left through an unmarked kissing gate.

Turn diagonally right past the corner of the garden and head for a kissing gate in the far left corner. Aim up the next three fields to Lapworth church and exit onto the road. Turn left and right into Tapster Lane and in 100 yards (90m) climb a stile on the left. Follow the hedge on the left to enter a private garden over a stile and bear

Lapworth

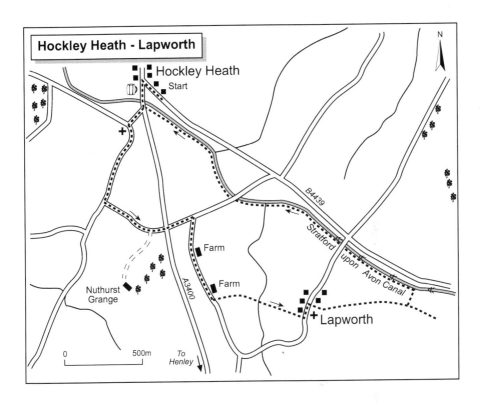

right along a mown path to pass the pond and exit over a stile. (Please remain on the path through the garden).

Go straight ahead up the field to a dog-leg hedge corner when it comes into view and climb the stile to continue to a kissing gate on the corner of the cricket field. Ignore the gate and turn left along the fence to join the canal in the field corner and cross the canal bridge. Turn left to follow the water on your left to bridge No. 25 and exit the towpath. Turn right through the car park of the Wharf Tavern and cross the main road to the war memorial and your car park is on the right.

Walk 5: Tanworth in Arden – Ladbrook Coppice

A walk to hold your interest to the very end with lovely homes and gardens along quiet country roads and a fine trail through Ladbrook Coppice. There are no cropped fields on the walk but care is needed at the live railway crossing. The Bell Inn is next to the church in Tanworth.

Distance: 5 miles (8km)
Allow: 2½ hours
Map: Ordnance Survey 1:25000 Explorer 220
Grid reference: 112704

How to get there:
From Coventry follow the B4101 through Knowle to Hockley Heath and turn left onto the A3400. After the Wharf Tavern, on the right,

Tamworth in Arden

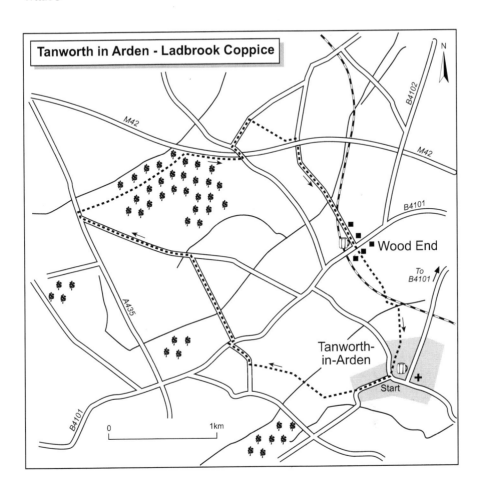

turn right into Spring Lane to continue on the B4101 for 2½ miles (4km). Turn left at the Tanworth sign and go on to the village to park at the roadside.

The route:
Walk through the village away from the church and turn left into Bates Lane, then follow it to a sharp left bend. Go forward into a green path at the kissing gate to enter a field and follow the hedge on your right to the corner. Turn right to the next gate and head for the footbridge ahead to continue up to a kissing gate. Go on between the fences to

exit at the stables and walk out to the road and turn right. At the main road, cross into Rushbrook Lane and follow it to the end. Turn left along Penn Lane for a half mile (800m) until the main road ahead comes into view and, at a large single house, turn right through a bridle gate ignoring the adjoining footpath. Follow the enclosed path into a spinney and enter the field on the right through a bridle gate to continue along the field edge to reach the wood. Enter the wood and immediately turn right to follow the well marked trail for a half mile (800m) to exit onto a track running parallel with the motorway.

Turn right to join the road and go ahead to the 40mph sign and in a few paces turn left over a stile. Follow the hedge on the right almost to the corner and turn right over a stile to go on with the hedge on the left to the end of the second field, then exit onto the road. Turn right and continue to the Old Royal Oak pub on the main road and cross carefully into a drive opposite with a sign for 'The Old Cottage'. Follow the enclosed path into a field and stay in the same direction to cross the railway line at the official crossing. Turn sharp left to cross a footbridge spanning the infant River Alne and go forward over the right hand stile to follow the hedge to the top corner of the field. In the next field continue on the other side of the hedge to enter an enclosed path and go on to the road. Turn left to return to the church and the Bell Inn.

Walk 6: Coundon Hall Park – Hawkes End

Strangers to this area may be surprised at the beauty of the countryside north west of Coventry where the footpath network is well maintained and waymarked by the Coventry Countryside Project.

Distance: 3½ miles (5.5km)
Allow: 1½ hours
Map: Ordnance Survey 1:25000 Explorer 221
Grid reference: 312819

How to get there:
From Coventry follow the B4098 Tamworth Road to the edge of the city and pass the Old Hall Hotel on the left. In a few more yards/metres, and just before the Royal Court Hotel on the right, turn left into the car park of the Coundon Hall sports field.

The Route:
With your back to the road, go ahead on the right side of the spinney and continue through a kissing gate. Veer right into the newly planted Coundon Wood and head for the far right corner to exit onto Long Lane and turn left to the island. Turn right into Wall Hill Road and fork right at the White Lion Inn to continue to a pylon in a field on the right. Turn left through a kissing gate and follow the fence on your right to the next kissing gate and aim for a pylon ahead.

Turn left along the drive for 65 yards (60m) and turn right into an enclosed path and exit into a paddock. Cross to a kissing gate and go over the track to continue on the left side of the house to join a lane. Go on to a row of bungalows and turn sharp right for a few paces to a farm. Follow the path past the buildings on the left and enter a field at the gate to follow the hedge on the right down to the road. Turn left for 70 yards (65m)and turn right through a kissing gate and go forward to the next gate and then turn sharp right to join the road. Cross into the path opposite and veer left to another gate and go ahead on the right side of an old hedgeline. In the next field follow

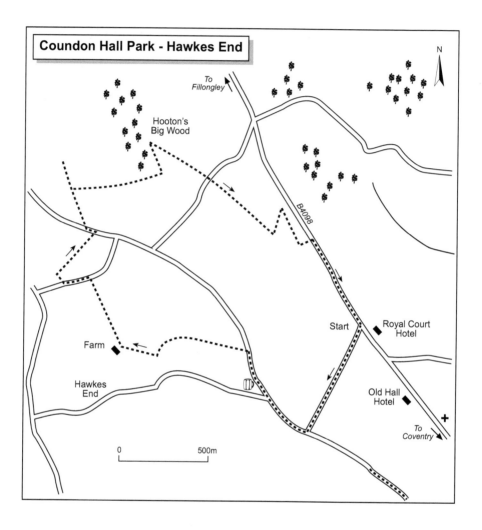

the hedge on the right for 100 yards (90m) and turn right at the kissing gate and go up to a drive. Cross into the drive opposite and pass through the yard to enter a field at the kissing gate. Turn left and follow the field edge for 100 yards (90m) and stop.

Turn right down the open field and descend to the kissing gate and a tall waymark post and climb the bank into the next field. Veer gently right up the open field to exit onto a lane and cross into the path opposite. Follow the fence on the left and maintain direction to the end of the next field and turn left behind the hedge. At the corner turn right to the next corner and turn left through a kissing gate bearing diagonally right to a gate adjoining the stable. Turn left to another gate and go out to the main road and turn right using the tarmac path opposite. Continue to the Royal Court Hotel on the left and cross with care into the sports field car park

Walk 7: Dunchurch – Thurlaston

Dunchurch was mentioned in the Domesday Book of 1086 and much of its history can be found around the village centre so take your time and look around. Along the way we visit Thurlaston and the hamlet of Toft each with a fine view across Draycote Water and you are sure to see scores of alpacas in their paddocks.

A sure to please walk for all the family.

Distance:	4½ miles (7.25km)
Allow:	2¼ hours
Map:	Ordnance Survey 1:25000 Explorer 222
Grid reference:	480709

Pudding Bag Lane - Thurlaston

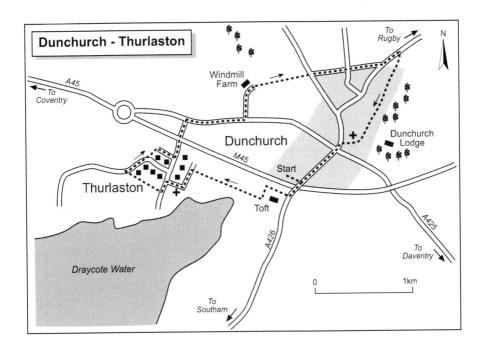

How to get there:

Follow the London Road A45 from Coventry to the centre of Dunchurch and turn right at the traffic lights. Go on to this side of the motorway bridge and turn right to park at this end of Sandford Way.

The Route:

Turn right along the main road and turn right into Toft Lane in 150 yards (135m). Follow the lane as it turns left between the gate pillars and climb a stile on the right. Descend the field parallel with the fence on the right and exit at a bridle gate. Go ahead over the service road and continue between the hedge and the fence to descend to a pair of bridle gates. Follow the hedge on your left to the corner and turn left through the yard to reach the church. Turn right to the junction and turn left past Pudding Bag Lane and in 50 yards (45m) turn right through a hand gate. Go on along the enclosed path to pass a private pond on the right and continue with a hedge on the right to join the road. Turn right to a sharp right bend and turn left over a stile next to a bench seat. Follow the narrow path to exit onto the end of a lane.

Turn right up the lane to the village stocks and turn left to the main road. Turn right for a ¼ mile (200m) and turn left into Windmill Lane and bear right at the farm as the lane becomes unsurfaced. Go on to join the main road and cross into Northampton Lane to continue past Alwyn Road on the left. At the end, turn left, crossing with care, and go on to about 200 yards (180m) short of a traffic island and enter a kissing gate on the right. Follow the enclosed path over the tree lined avenue of Bilton Grange and in 25 yards (23m) enter the field on the right at a kissing gate. Go on with the hedge on the left and maintain direction to exit at the road next to the entrance gates to Dunchurch Park. Walk on along Vicarage Lane for 50 yards (45m) and turn left into a narrow path to continue through the churchyard and exit at the centre of Dunchurch with Guy Fawkes' House to the left and a statue of Lord John Scott to the right. Follow the Southam Road to return to your car.

Walk 8: Fillongley – Square Lane

The two streams still run through Fillongley, so essential to the two castles which stood here. Alas there is little evidence of either castle today but we will see the few remaining stones of the de-Hastings castle on the walk. Try to imagine the castle in its heyday as you pass by.

Distance: 3½ miles (5.5km)
Allow: 1½ hours
Map: Ordnance Survey 1:25000 Explorer 221
Grid reference: 281872

How to get there:
From Coventry follow the Tamworth Road B4098 to Fillongley and turn right into Church Lane and park neatly.

The Route:
Return to the main road and cross to the left side of the newsagents opposite. Walk past the garages to a stile and turn right down the steps to enter a field. Turn left along the stream and then turn left through a kissing gate to pass the remains of the de-Hastings castle on the right. Follow the fence on the left to a hand gate and footplank and turn left into a large field.

Stay on the field edge to reach the opposite side of the field and proceed with the hedge on the left towards the distant motorway. Continue over a narrow strip of field to a stile and bear gently left to a pond hidden by bushes. Go on with a hedge on the left to cross a footbridge and continue to the end of the hedge on your right. Climb a stile in the wire fence in front and turn sharp left along the fence to a culverted stream at the end of the field.

Go ahead up the fields with the hedge on the right to reach a pond at the top and continue through the gate in the holly hedge. Veer left to the right side of the house and exit onto the main road and turn right down the hill. At the Saracens Head pub turn left into Square Lane

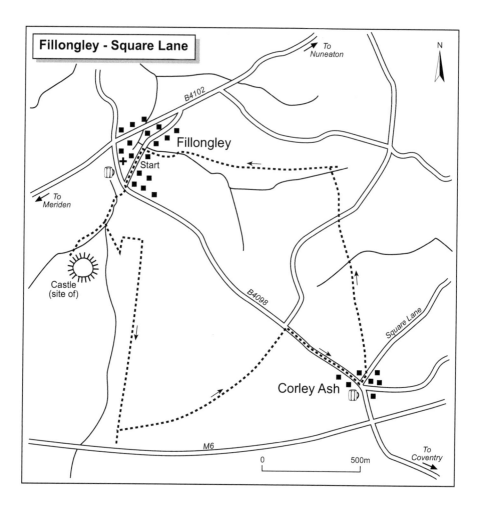

and in 120 yards (110m) turn left through a field gate. Head up the middle of the field to a hand gate and go on past a private plantation on the left. Just before the private lake enter the adjoining field on the right and follow the field edge to a waymark post which we ignore. Go on to another waymark post at the corner of the hedgeline and bear gently right to a kissing gate.

Head up the next field veering right to join the road and cross to the gate a little to your left. Turn diagonally right to the next gate and descend with the hedge on the left to enter a narrow field through a gate. Turn left and follow the hedge on the right to a farm track and cross into the next field. Descend with the hedge on the right to cross a footbridge and cross the open field to its left corner and enter the sports field. Go ahead along the hedge on the left to return to Church Lane and turn left to your car.

Walk 9: Mickleton – The Hidcotes

Mickleton is an edge of Cotswold village surrounded by beautiful countryside and just a stones throw from the famous gardens of Kiftsgate and Hidcote. Be prepared for a gentle one mile (1.6km) climb to Hidcote Manor.

This sure to please walk is well way marked and the two Hidcotes will leave you with pleasant memories.

Distance: 4 miles (6.5km)
Allow: 2 hours
Map: Ordnance Survey 1:25000 Explorer 205
Grid reference: 160435

How to get there:
From Coventry follow the A423 to Princethorpe and turn right onto the Fosse Way and continue through Halford. Turn first right at the Armscote sign and go on to Ilmington, then turn right along Front Street and left onto the Mickleton Road. At the village centre pass the Three Ways Hotel on the right and park in the vicinity of the church on the left.

The Route:
Enter the lane leading to the church and follow it to its end ignoring other paths on the right. Go through the bridle gate where the path divides into three ways and go straight ahead to an iron kissing gate. Head through the middle of the next field to a stile and climb the incline to the next stile. Go on past the yellow marker post to the far corner of the fenced off conifers and veer left to descend to the field corner with Kiftsgate Court high up on the left.

Climb the next field to the Kiftsgate gate pillars and exit onto the road, then go forward along the lane to Hidcote. Turn right along the lane in front of the National Trust car park and follow it to its end. Enter the track ahead and stay in the same direction to a stile at the bottom of the field. Head up the middle of the field to the farm, when it comes

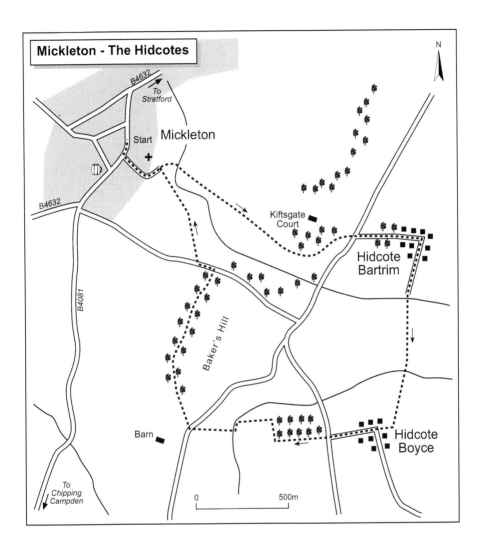

into view, and join the road at Hidcote Boyce. Walk on through the
village to the main road and cross to a field gate opposite to enter an
enclosed footpath. Enter a field at the bottom and turn right to the
corner and turn left to the next corner and cross a footbridge a few
paces to the left. Head up the field with the hedge on the left to a
narrow lane and cross to the barn opposite. Ignore the track ahead
and immediately turn right along the field edge to enter a spinney and

On The Way To Mickleton

follow the trail to exit into a field. Go on to a bridle gate and stile in the field corner and descend to the road but beware of traffic. Cross to the bridle gate and head down the field to cross a footbridge in the far right corner and turn left through a bridle gate. Follow the path to return to the church and turn right into the village.

Walk 10: Yarningale Common – Preston Bagot

The ever popular Yarningale Common opens the walk which ends with a meandering mile (1km) along the infant River Alne. In between we go to Preston Bagot and its church of All Saints built by the Normans to look over a panorama of open countryside, unchanged to the present day. Attractive scenery throughout the walk.

Distance:	3½ miles (5.5km)
Allow:	1 hour 30 minutes
Map:	Ordnance Survey 1:25000 Explorer 220
Grid reference:	189658

How to get there:
From Coventry follow the A46 to the Solihull exit A4177 and go on through Hatton. After the Waterman Inn fork left onto the B4439 and in 1½ miles (2.4km) fork left to Shrewley. Turn left through the village and after the Ardencote Country Club on the left, turn second right at the Yarningale sign and turn right down Common Lane. Park around the common in the parking bays.

The Route:
With your back to Common Lane follow Ossetts Hole Lane for a half mile (800m) to Claverdon Rugby Club and go on for 150 yards (135m) and turn right at a waymark post. Follow the path through the bushes and enter a field at a gate. Aim through the centre of the field to a gap in the tree line to reach the canal and cross the footbridge into a spinney. Follow the trail over a footbridge and enter a field at a hand gate. Go up the hedge on the left to the corner and in the next field veer left to a kissing gate at the roadside.

Cross the road into the church drive and go on to the far end of the churchyard wall and turn right to a large farmhouse. Go ahead through the right hand gate to follow the hedge on the left to reach a stile beneath a dead tree. Ignore the stile and turn right into the enclosed path and go on to exit into a field, then follow the hedge on

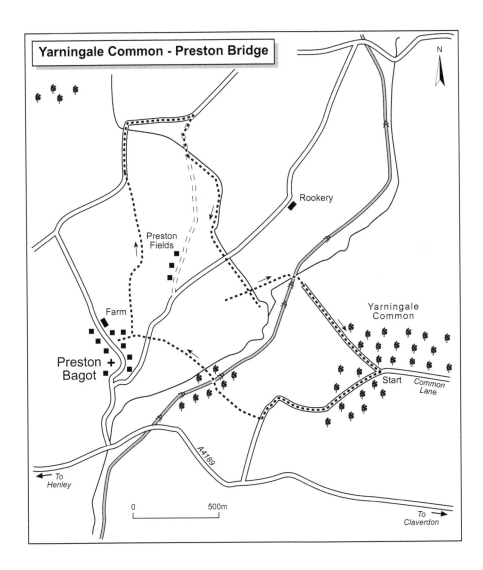

Yarningale Common - Preston Bridge

N

Rookery

Preston
Fields

Farm

Yarningale
Common

Preston
Bagot

Start   Common
Lane

A4189

To
Henley

0   500m

To
Claverdon

the left to join the lane next to the red brick house. Turn left and continue as the lane becomes unsurfaced and descend to this side of the ford to turn right over a stile. With the river on your left, continue through the fields to reach a lane and cross to the opposite stile. Proceed along the river to a large footbridge and turn left. Veer right off the footbridge to a hand gate in the corner and enter the spinney to exit into a field with tall grasses. Don't be deterred but follow the trail as it veers left to reach a stile at the foot of the canal bank. Climb the steps onto the canal towpath and turn right for a few paces to cross the canal over a footbridge. Turn left on the other side of the canal and in 40 yards (37m) turn right down the steps. Go out to the lane and follow it back to the common.

Yarningale Common

Walk 11: Chesterton – Bunkers Hill

Chesterton has always been a magnet for ramblers, perhaps because of its remoteness. There are no shops or pubs, just an historic church alone in the fields to serve a few farms and cottages. In days past the community must have been much larger with Peyto's Manor House adjoining the church, hence the restored gateway in the churchyard wall used only by the Peyto family. Alas all that remains of the manor is the garden wall. The Kingston Estate roads form most of the route with just two arable fields to cross at the end of the walk.

Distance: 4 miles (6.5km)
Allow: 2 hours
Map: Ordnance Survey 1:25000 Explorer 206
Grid reference: 347585

St. Giles church – Chesterton

How to get there:
From Coventry follow the A423 to Princethorpe and turn right onto the Fosse Way. In nine miles (14.5km) turn left into Windmill Hill Lane at the Chesterton sign just before the crossing of the M40. In one mile (1.6km) turn right into the village and park in the vicinity of the Old Gated Road.

The Route:
Follow the church sign along the lane and pass the church on the left. Continue through the gate pillars of Kingston Farm and go on to the walled manor house on the right where the road divides. Turn left to the farm in a half mile (800m) and at the far end of the farm buildings turn left in front of the house and continue to a small wood on your right. Turn right into the wood and follow the trail as it bears left to rejoin the road through a bridle gate and cross over to go through a double field gate a few yards/metres ahead.

Follow the hedge on the right into the third field and pass the houses

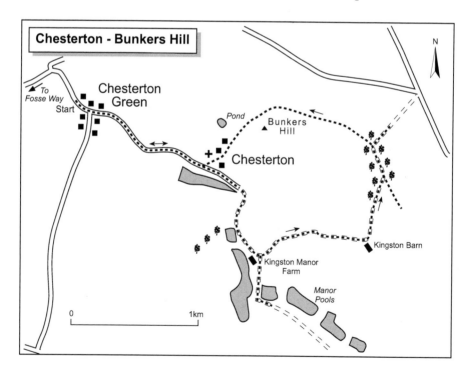

to reach a field gate on the right giving access to the road. Turn sharp left down the field and veer gently to the right to pass well to the left of a pond, when it comes into view, and go on to climb a stile in the hedgeline. There is a small copse to your left. Go straight ahead in the next field to a redundant stile next to a drainage ditch and swing diagonally right to join the road through a kissing gate in the field corner. Turn right to return to your car.

Walk 12: Wimpstone – Crimscote

On the outward leg of this walk the lonely church of St Mary at Whitchurch can be seen in the fields on the left but the village disappeared long ago. The novelist Ursula Bloom wrote of Whitchurch where her father was the rector. On the other side of the River Stour, Alderminster Church has stood for over 700 years. Here in the 14th Century every inhabitant died from the Black Death.

A good walk to avoid ploughed fields and stiles.

Distance:	4 miles (6.5km)
Allow:	2 hours
Map:	Ordnance Survey 1:25000 Explorer 205
Grid reference:	213491

How to get there:
Follow the A46 from Coventry to Stratford and turn left over the river. Turn right onto the A3400 and continue for almost four miles (6.4km) and turn right at the sign for Wimpstone. Park next to the river bridge without obstructing the gate.

The Route:
Walk on along the lane and fork left at the Crimscote sign. Remain on the picturesque lane for almost two miles (3.2km) to reach the Crimscote village sign and turn left through the kissing gate. Bear diagonally left in the meadow with the winding river to your right and pass through another kissing gate. Stay in the same direction to cross the river footbridge and go up to the main road. Turn left, using the pavement at all times, to pass Alderminster Church and then the Bell Inn and continue past a row of estate cottages on the left.

After the last cottage look for the easily missed footpath on your left and follow it to the bottom of the grass bank and turn right. Stay on the trail as it climbs to the top of the bank and enters a spinney and go on parallel with the road to exit into a field and climb the stile. Go forward for 90 yards (80m) and cross a concrete farm bridge before

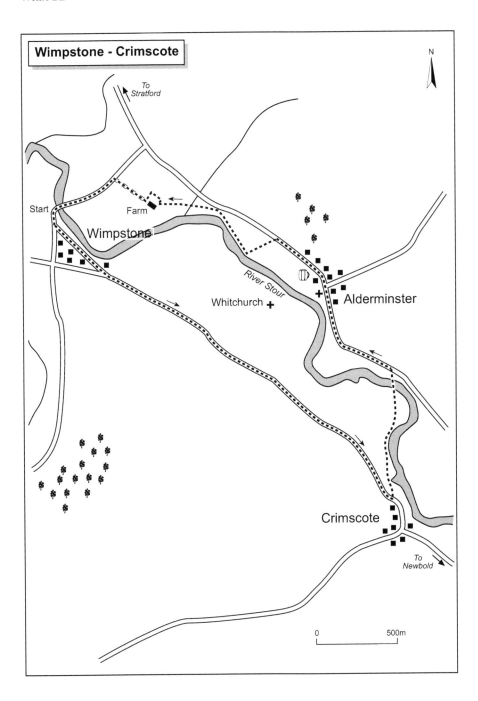

swinging left to the field corner on the right side of the farm. Exit at the field gate and cross the farm drive into the field and follow the garden fence on your left. Join the farm drive on the left and follow it to the road and turn left to return to your car.

Walk 13: Hartshill Hayes – The Outwoods

This fine family walk offers a beautiful woodland walk, a spectacular working quarry and a country park with views across four counties. Enjoy this one in any season.

Distance: 4 miles (6.5km)
Allow: 2 hours
Map: Ordnance Survey 1:25000 Explorer 232
Grid reference: 317943

How to get there:
From Nuneaton follow the B4114 to a crossroads at Chapel End and turn right into Victoria Road. Turn right along Church Road and then left into Oldbury Road and the country park is on the right. There is an all day parking fee. Note the closing time at the entrance.

The Route:
Enter the trail on the left side of the children's playground with the reservoir fence on your left. Stay on the higher path and turn left where the fence turns left and exit through the park gates. Go forward along the road to pass Oldbury Grange on the left and then The Lodge on the right and in a further 100 yards (90m) turn right into a waymarked path. Follow the path as it turns to the right to reveal views of the quarry and turn left at a waymark post. Continue up the enclosed path to the road and turn left into the path parallel with the road. At the end cross the road to the left side of the Purley Chase church centre and enter the path to proceed straight ahead through the centre of the wood to reach the road.

Turn left for 100 yards (90m) and turn left through a kissing gate to cross the golf fairway and descend to a footbridge. Stay close to the treeline on your left and follow the waymark to the next kissing gate. Head up the hill veering right to the corner beyond the farm and behind the line of fine oak trees. Climb a stile onto the farm track and turn left to continue to the road. Cross into the bridle path and turn

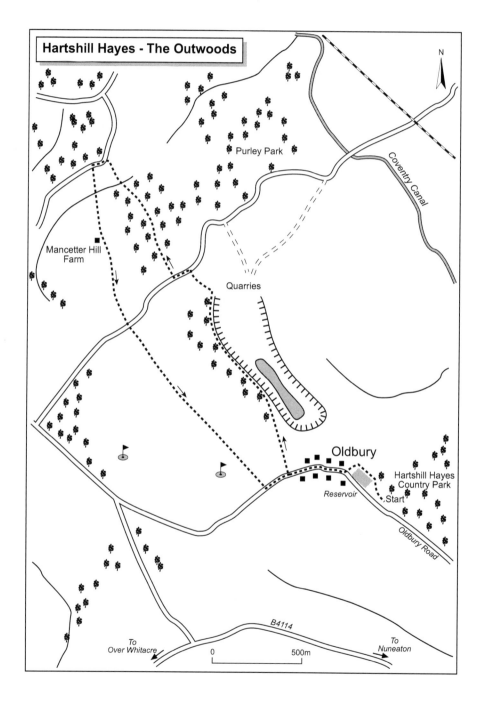

Hartshill Hayes - The Outwoods

N

Purley Park

Coventry Canal

Mancetter Hill
Farm

Quarries

Oldbury

Hartshill Hayes
Country Park

Reservoir

Start

Oldbury Road

B4114

To
Over Whitacre

To
Nuneaton

0   500m

left and right through the nursery buildings to pass the pond on your right. Go straight ahead to enter the golf course and bear left for 30 yards (27m) to a waymark post. Turn right and stay in the same direction following the markers across the golf course, remaining alert to the golfers. Join the road at a kissing gate and turn left to return to the country park where you made the earlier exit. Bear right to return to the car park.

Hartshill Hayes

Walk 14: Wroxhall – Hay Wood

Wroxall is a tiny hamlet with a magical past. Here stood a mansion on the site of the ruins of an abbey bought by Sir Christopher Wren after the completion of St Pauls. Still remaining from Sir Christopher's time is the parkland with avenues of oak trees and the garden with ancient cedars. Around the garden is a wall built by the great man himself. The final part of the walk is through the delightful Hay Wood.

Distance: 4 miles (6.5km)
Allow: 2 hours
Map: Ordnance Survey 1:25000 Explorer 221
Grid reference: 224713

How to get there:
Follow the A46 from Coventry and exit at the Solihull sign onto the A4177 and continue through Hatton for three miles (4.8km) to a large island. Join the A4141 to Wroxall and turn second right into Manor Lane and park in School Lane on the left.

The Route:
Enter a short footpath adjoining the school playing field and go ahead over the main road, taking great care, into the farm track. Go ahead on the track with the fence on the right to reach the first waymark post and turn sharp left to pass the pond on your left and aiming for the corner of Wren's wall. Go on along the tarmac path to cross the main entrance of the hotel and walk on to enter a field through a kissing gate. Stay in the same direction along the treeline on your right to the corner and exit at the kissing gate to go ahead to join the lane. Turn right to Mousley Hill Cottage on the left in just under a ¼ mile (400m) and turn right into a waymarked drive. Proceed through the yard with the hedge on the left and exit in the corner at a kissing gate.

Go on with the hedge on your right to pass the pond and in the next field head down the centre to a stile in the left corner. Follow the hedge on the left to cross a stile and footbridge and continue through

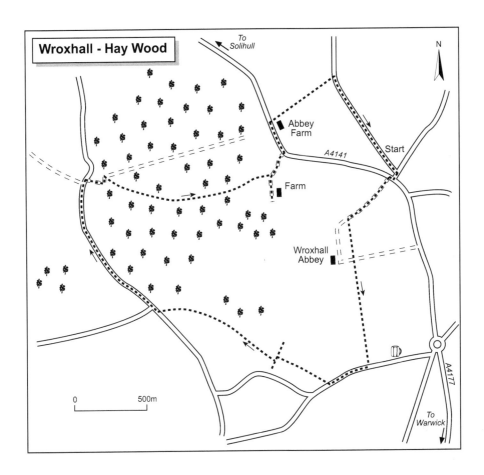

the centre of the next field curving to the left to exit onto the lane. Turn right and remain on the lane for ¾ mile (1.2km) to reach a drive on the left leading to the National Trust's Baddesley Clinton Manor. Turn right through the field gate and go ahead to enter Hay Wood. Turn left for 30 yards (27m) to a field gate on the left and turn sharp right to follow the bridle path through the middle of the wood. Maintain direction over a crossroad of paths and as you near the end of the wood exit through a waymarked bridle gate into a field. Aim for a field gate next to the barns and go forward onto a farm track. Turn left onto the farm drive and follow it to the main road and turn left using the pavement. Go on to Abbey Farm on the right and follow

Wroxall

the drive turning left and right through the buildings to enter a fenced
bridle path and follow it to the lane. Turn right to return to your car.

Walk 15: New End – Cookhill

Perhaps one of the most attractive walks you will ever do in the midland counties with magnificent views to the Malvern and Clee Hills in the west and beautiful Warwickshire to the east. Our starting point is the Nevill Arms on the historic Ridgeway at its junction with the equally ancient Saltway. Food and drink is available daily at the pub.

Distance: 5 miles (8km)
Allow: 2½ hours
Map: Ordnance Survey 1:25000 Explorer 205/220
Grid reference: 050600

How to get there:
From Coventry follow the A46 to the outskirts of Alcester and turn left onto the A422. Follow it as it turns sharp right to reach the A441 and turn right for two miles (32.km) to the Nevill Arms on the left where walkers have permission to park.

The Route:
Walk along the Saltway and turn left into Brandheath Lane and at a private gateway across your path, turn right. Stay in the same direction to the bottom field with a pylon and go forward over the footbridge to continue through the fields to join a lane. Cross into the next path and follow the hedge on the left to an underground gas station and enter the next field. Follow the right field edge for 150 yards (135m) and change sides with the hedge to continue to a lane. Turn right for a good quarter mile (400m) and just before the farm, turn left at a waymarked field gate and go ahead with the stream on your right to the end of the second field, ignoring the footbridge. Turn left up the hedge and climb the stile and turn right into the corner.

Turn left and descend to a culverted ditch a little to the left and go ahead past a pylon to reach a farm road. Turn left and in a few paces turn right through a storage yard and climb the stile in the right corner. Continue with the hedge on the right to a footbridge at the

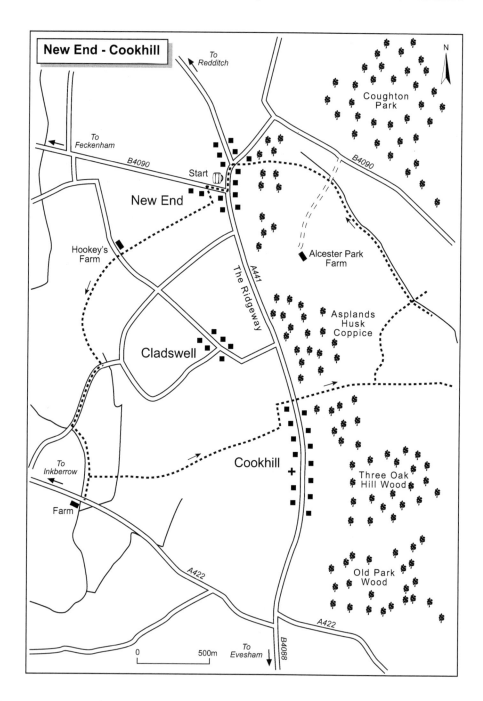

end of the second field and veer to the right hedgeline and follow it into the village. Turn left at the crossroads until the road ends and turn right into a waymarked path and go out to the main road.

Cross to the bridle path and go ahead to the end of the wood on the left and enter the enclosed path ahead. Continue along the right field edge to a waymark post at the field corner and turn left. Stay with the hedge on your right around many angles to reach a culverted field entrance with a waymark. Turn right into the corner and turn left to the next corner. Turn left and ignore the footbridge to follow the hedge on the right to a double power pole at a waymark post. Veer left and follow the hedge on your left to exit onto a farm road and cross into a track and head up to the corner of the wood. Turn left and then right on this side of the barn and follow the trail to a stile in the left corner. In a few paces enter a field over another stile and turn left to the stile in the corner. Go ahead through a spinney to exit on the main road opposite the Nevill Arms.

Walk 16: Hampton in Arden – Barston

A walk guaranteed to hold your interest to the end and very easy to follow. Long ago Hampton was at the heart of the great Forest of Arden and its history goes back long before the Norman Conquest. The old church in the High Street has already celebrated its 850th anniversary and is surrounded by houses from the 17th century to the present day. Along the way is the beautiful hamlet of Walsal End and later we pass the packhorse bridge, a mere 500 years old.

Distance: 4½ miles (7,25km)
Allow: 2¼ hours
Map: Ordnance Survey 1:25000 Explorer 221
Grid reference: 203813

How to get there:
Go to Meriden from Coventry and follow Hampton Lane B4102 to the village centre and cross the railway bridge. Turn right into Shadow Brook Lane and park at the sports centre.

The Route:
Return to the main road and turn right to the church. Cross carefully at the corner into Bell Vue Terrace and on the right corner enter the waymarked path behind a hedge and follow it into a field. With the hedge on the left continue through two fields, then cross the footbridge and go ahead to cross a farm road. Go on in the same direction over the open field to enter Walsal End over a stile and turn left. Continue on a waymarked track between the timber framed cottages, ignoring the lane on your right.

Stay on the track as it turns left and in 20 yards (18m) climb a stile on your right. Veer left over the open field and at the bottom cross a footbridge and go forward to a stile when it comes into view. Bear slight left to the next stile and turn left behind the hedge to continue over a pair of stiles and exit onto the road in Barston. Turn right and then left to pass the Bulls Head and walk to the end of the village.

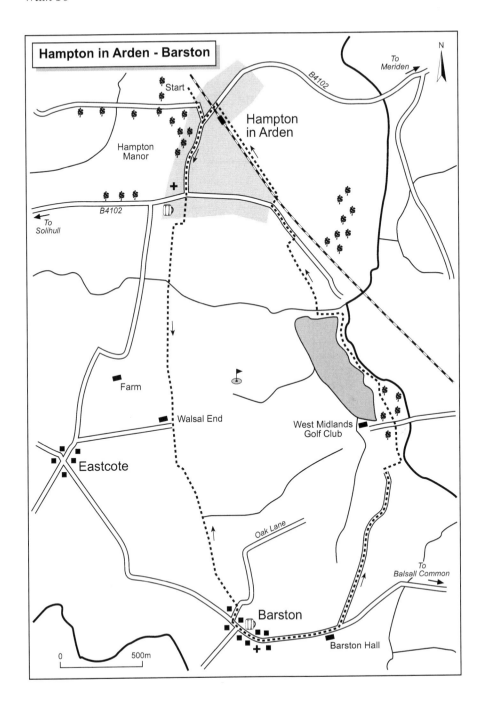

Hampton in Arden - Barston

Start

B4102

To
Meriden

N

Hampton
in Arden

Hampton
Manor

B4102

To
Solihull

Farm

Walsal End

West Midlands
Golf Club

Eastcote

Oak Lane

To
Balsall Common

0   500m

Barston

Barston Hall

Turn first left into Ryton End and stay on the lane as it becomes a bridle path, which is followed until reaching West Midlands Golf Club. Turn right to the wrought iron gates and turn left at the waymark post to reach the end of the lake with the car park on your left. Go ahead with the lake on the left to fishing peg No. 69 and turn right on the shale path to exit onto Marsh Lane. Turn left and, halfway along the lane, turn right beneath the railway and turn left along the foot of the embankment. At the end turn left over the railway bridge and turn right to the main road in Hampton. Cross with care to the footpath opposite which leads back to the car park.

Bradnocks Marsh - Hampton In Arden

Walk 17: Golf Drive – Burton Hastings

A cool breeze blows across this flat arable landscape, ideal for a walk on those hot summer days. We soon cross the River Anker at Pauls Ford remembered by past generations as a beauty spot where they played and paddled all day long. Alas some of the distant views are marred by the encroaching garish buildings. On the return leg we visit the delightful village of Burton Hastings.

Distance: 5 miles (8km)
Allow: 2½ hours
Map: Ordnance Survey 1:25000 Explorer 232
Grid reference: 384899

How to get there:
Golf Drive is two miles (3.2km) south east of Nuneaton town centre on the Wolvey Road B4114 or access from Bedworth is along Gipsy Lane. Park at the far end of Golf Drive.

The Route:
Go ahead down the farm road to a kissing gate and turn left for 100 yards (90m). Turn right and follow the track over the River Anker at Pauls Ford and continue for one mile (1.6km) to the waymark posts where a staggered footpath crosses your path. Turn right and follow the hedge on the left until the track divides and turn sharp left to an old iron barn. Veer right across the open field to a hedge corner and go on along the field edge to cross a footbridge. Head straight across the open field to the right side of a clump of trees and turn right along the raised path. Follow it as it turns left for 120 yards (110m) and turn right over a farm bridge and head up to the village.

Turn right through the village to a road junction and turn right to continue forward along Mill Lane, passing the church on your right. Go on to a stable and paddock on the left and a farm on the right and around the next bend enter a waymarked field gate on your right. Turn left and follow the track over the canal bridge and in 100 yards (90m)

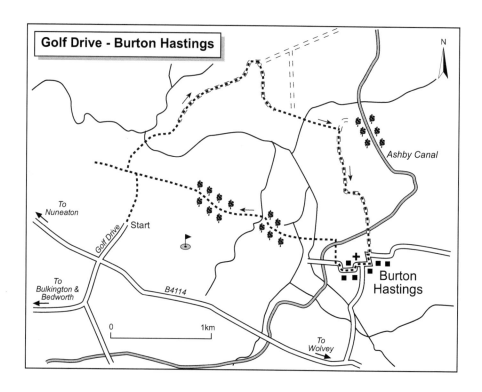

turn left. Stay in this direction to cross an open field and climb a waymarked fence stile. Go forward for a few paces to a kissing gate on the left and follow the trail through a spinney with the golf course to the left. Exit into a field and turn left ignoring a path on the right and walk on to a footbridge. Veer diagonally right across the open field to the corner and enter the spinney adjoining the golf course fence and follow the trail into a field. Stay in the same direction to reach a pair of waymark posts and go ahead through the kissing gate to follow the hedge on the left past the farm, also on the left, and descend to the kissing gate used on the outward journey. Turn left to return to your car.

Walk 18: Hampton in Arden – Ryton End

Here is a walk to show some of the hidden corners of the lovely historic village of Hampton. We also visit the lake at Ryton End, home of the West Midland Golf Club, once a massive quarry but now a mecca for golfers, walkers and fishermen and of course home to a variety of water birds.

Distance: 5 miles (8km)
Allow: 2½ hours
Map: Ordnance Survey 1:25000 Explorer 221
Grid reference: 203813

How to get there:
From Meriden follow the Hampton Road B4102 to the centre of the village and cross the railway bridge. Turn right into Shadow Brook Lane and turn right into the Hampton Sports Centre car park.

The Route:
Return to the main road on the path next to the railway fence and cross into Station Road. Turn left over the railway bridge and then right for 15 yards (14m) and turn left into a narrow path at a barrier. Follow the path over two residential roads and climb a stile into a field. Turn right to about halfway down the field and turn left on a well used path and follow it as it turns left to continue between a pair of hedges. At the end climb the stile on your right and in a few paces turn left on the hedge corner for 25 yards (23m). Turn right and veer left to a kissing gate to gain access to the road and turn right over the river bridge using the pavement opposite. After crossing the bridge, carefully cross the road to follow the narrow verge past the farm to a footpath signpost and turn right through a kissing gate. Follow the redundant road straight ahead and pass a lorry park on the right.

Remain on the road as it turns right and continue to the railway bridge and turn left onto a farm drive. Go ahead over the stile and follow the railway embankment to the end of the second field and turn right to

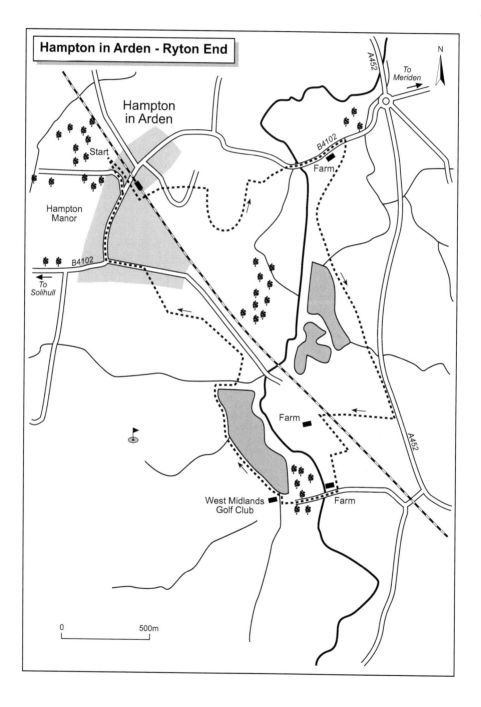

the corner. Climb the stile and go forward along the field edge to join the road. Turn right and after crossing the River Blythe turn right at the footpath signpost next to the gates of the golf club. Follow the path for a few yards/metres to this end of the lake and turn left to circle the lake on your right to reach fishing peg No. 69. Exit onto a wide shale path at a stout waymark post and follow it to just before the exit onto Marsh Lane. Turn left through the hedge at the hand rails and go on through the middle of three fields on a well used path to enter a narrow path between the houses. At the road, turn left to the end of the road and climb the stile on your right. Go forward over the adjoining stile and head for the far left corner to exit onto Marsh Lane and turn left. At the church turn right to return to Shadow Brook Lane.

Packhorse Bridge – Hampton in Arden

Walk 19: Farnborough – Mollington

A great family walk centred on the National Trust's Farnborough Hall and the beautiful village of Mollington. The Holbech family purchased the hall and estates in 1684 and so became Lords of the Manor of both villages with the obelisk built as a focal point between the two. The family name can be seen on memorials in the churches of each village. A noisy half mile (800m) of motorway is soon forgotten as you head into glorious countryside. There is a nice pub in each village.

Distance:	4½ miles (7.25km)
Allow:	2¼ hours
Map:	Ordnance Survey 1:25000 Explorer 206
Grid reference:	429494

How to get there:

Follow the A423 from Coventry to Southam and turn left onto the bypass. Continue ahead on the A423 to pass the Wharf Inn on the right and in two miles (3.2km) turn right at the Farnborough sign. In the village pass Forge Lane on the right and fork right on the lower road to bear left along Dassett Road and the car park is on the right.

The Route:

Turn right out of the car park and turn first left into a lane or use the woodland path parallel with the road to reach the lane. Follow the lane to the motorway bridge and turn left over a stile and descend the steps to continue on the path to a stile on the county border. Go ahead to a waymark post and descend diagonally left to the corner of the barn and then pass through a waymarked hedge gap in the corner. Follow the stream on your left to the end of the second field and stop at a group of tall conifers and a metal farm bridge.

Ignore the bridge and turn right along the stream for 50 yards (45m) and cross a wooden footbridge to go straight ahead through the middle of the field to a waymarked hedge gap. Turn left behind the hedge and continue into Mollington. Walk up the hill or use the raised

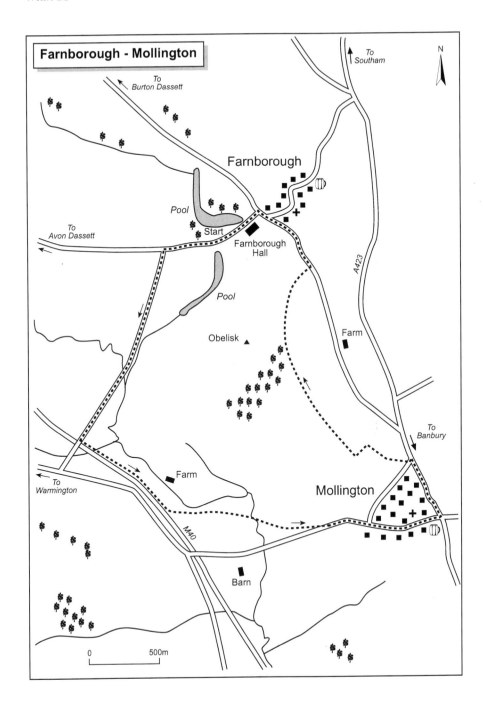

Farnborough - Mollington

Farnborough Hall

path on your left to proceed through the village until just before the Green Man Inn.

Turn left at the church sign to enter the churchyard on your right and follow the path to the exit. Turn left and go ahead over the private lawn without lingering and climb the stile in front to continue past the paddocks on the right. Cross a narrow lane and go on with the hedge on the right, maintaining direction through the centre of the next field. Remain in the same direction to reach a bridle gate on the farm drive or, if more convenient, use the left field edge. Enter the bridle gate and follow the wood on your left to reach the National Trust's property. Turn diagonally right through the parkland and continue until the right end of the estate wall comes into view and exit onto the road. Turn left and return to the car park by bearing left.

Walk 20: Wootton Wawen – Five Acre Wood

Historic Wootton Wawen is the perfect place to begin this wonderful scenic walk. The beautiful old church stands next to Wootton Hall where the Prince Regent lived with Mrs Maria Fitzherbert before ascending to the throne as George IV.

Distance:	5½ miles (9km)
Allow:	2 hours 30 minutes
Map:	Ordnance Survey 1:25000 Explorer 220
Grid reference:	150631

How to get there:
From Coventry follow the A46 over the Longbridge island and turn first right at the Norton Lindsey sign. Turn first left and continue

Wootton Hall – Wootton Wawen

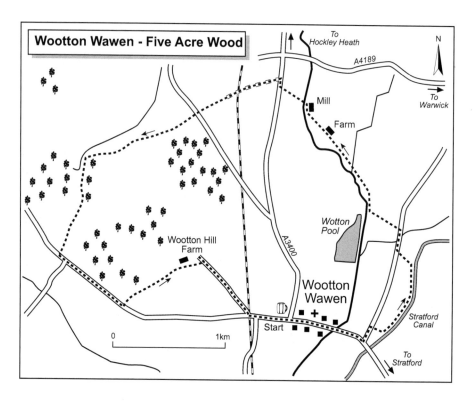

ahead for six miles (9.5km) to the Golden Cross on the A3400. Turn right to Wootton Wawen and fork left to park at the village hall opposite the Bulls Head.

The Route:
Walk through the village to pass the church on the left and continue to Pettiford Lane and turn left. In 200 yards (180m) turn right into a lane leading to Lucy's Farm opposite Yew Tree Farm Craft Centre. Turn left along the canal towpath to reach bridge No. 51 and exit along the track on your left to join the road. Turn right to cross the river bridge and in 65 yards (60m) enter a kissing gate on the left and cross the open field diagonally right to reach the river. Bear right along the river bank until the path divides at a waymark post but continue along the river to exit at a farm gate. Turn left down the drive and at the far end of the mill turn sharp right and cross a footbridge. Follow the trail to exit into a school playing field and turn right and left around the

perimeter to exit onto a main road. Turn right for 100 yards (90m), then turn left into the drive of Warwickshire College and follow it over the railway bridge. Enter a hand gate on the left and turn right to a similar gate, then go forward to another gate. Maintain direction through a kissing gate and descend to the road.

Cross to the path opposite and go ahead past the farm buildings on your right to the end of the field and turn right into a track next to a pond. Remain on the track to enter a field through the right hand gate and follow the hedge on the left to the corner. Turn left at the kissing gate and in the next field head for the hedge on the left and follow it to a field gate. Go forward along the cart track to join the road. Turn left to reach Park House on the left and in a few paces turn left over a stile, then go ahead for 100 yards (90m) to climb the stile on your right. Remain in the same direction on the other side of the fence to the top of the field and cross the stile a few paces to the right. Veer to the left side of the field and descend to climb a stile on the left. Circle the pond to another stile and turn left to descend to a lane and turn right to a road junction. Turn left under the railway bridge to return to the Bulls Head.

Walk 21: Priors Hardwick – Upper Boddington

Priors Hardwick is a beautiful, peaceful village whose beginnings are lost in time but we know that some of the roads were laid down over a thousand years ago. In the 16th century the village was cleared by the Prior of Coventry to accommodate the grazing of sheep and evidence still exists of the deserted village in the field behind St Mary's church.

A lovely scenic route in two counties with a nice pub at the end of walk.

Distance: 4½ miles (7.25km)
Allow: 2¼ hours
Map: Ordnance Survey 1:25000 Explorer 206
Grid reference: 471561

How to get there:
Follow the A423 from Coventry to the Southam bypass and turn left at an island onto the A425. Immediately turn right at the Priors Hardwick sign and continue over a canal bridge. Turn first right and follow the sign to the village centre and park in the area of the church and the Butchers Arms.

The Route:
Walk past the Butchers Arms to pass the first lane on the left and at the next bend turn left into a waymarked farm drive. Enter the field at the hand gate and climb the hill staying close to the drive to reach a waymark post next to the farmhouse. Swing left to a kissing gate and turn right along the refurbished hedge on the right to the corner. Ignore the bridle gate on your right. Turn left for 45 yards (40m) and turn right behind the hedge and go forward over a stile through two fields to a sleeper bridge between a pair of stiles. Go ahead up the hill to the next stile and continue with the hedge on the right through two fields. Maintain direction over the open field to another sleeper bridge and cross the next field diagonally right to the opposite corner. Exit onto a wide bridle path and go ahead for 50 yards (45m) and turn right through a field gate to follow the fence on the left to the corner.

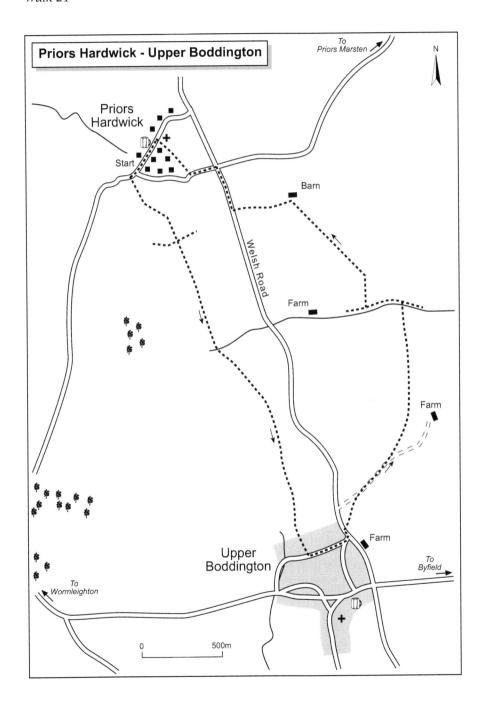

Priors Hardwick - Upper Boddington

To Priors Marsten

N

Priors Hardwick

Start

Barn

Welsh Road

Farm

Farm

Farm

Upper Boddington

To Byfield

To Wormleighton

0   500m

Priors Hardwick

Go ahead through the middle gate and descend to the end of the second field and climb the stile a little to your right. Head for the stile at the rear of the houses and go out to the road in Upper Boddington and turn left to a junction.

Walk on for 50 yards (45m) to the main road and turn left for 150 yards (135m) and enter a kissing gate on the right. Cross diagonally left to a similar gate and join the farm road in front of the stable (the proper route stays in this field to exit at a kissing gate in the bottom left corner). Continue on the farm road to a cattle grid where the road descends to a farm and stop. Turn left behind the hedge for a few paces and turn right down the centre of the field to a footbridge and bear left to another footbridge. Cross the next two fields in the same direction to the next footbridge and step into Warwickshire. Turn left to the corner and pass through two adjoining bridle gates onto a bridle path and turn sharp right with the hedge on the right to the corner. In the next field cross diagonally left to the distant barn crossing a stile as you go and exit at a field gate. Cross the track to a field gate on the left and in the next field follow the hedge on the right to about halfway up the field. Veer left to a field gate and turn right along the road to a crossroads. Turn left into London End and in 150 yards (135m) enter a kissing gate on the right and head for the left side of the church. Pass through the kissing gate and over a footbridge to enter the churchyard. Turn left to exit at the lychgate.

Walk 22: Monks Kirby – Pailton

The Newnham Paddox estate came to the Fielding family in the 15th Century as the seat of the Earls of Denbigh but, alas, the grand house was demolished in 1952. Our walk takes us over the estate lands in exquisite countryside to Pailton where Lady Mary Fielding lived at Pailton Hall. The walk is entirely over cropped fields best undertaken in a dry summer period when the paths have been well padded by previous walkers, but the great enjoyment of the walk is due to the farmers who ensure their footpaths are always clear.

Distance: 4½ miles (7.25km)
Allow: 2¼ hours
Map: Ordnance Survey 1:25000 Explorer 222
Grid reference: 467831

How to get there:
An easy route from Coventry is via Brinklow and Stretton under Fosse to Monks Kirby. In the village follow Brockhurst Lane to the end of the village and park neatly.

The Route:
The walk begins in the 'No Through Road' on the right. Look for a waymarked track on the right before reaching the entrance to Newnham Paddox and follow it straight ahead through the centre of the field with the parkland to the left. Continue through a hedgeline and stay in the same direction to reach a farm bridge on your right but do not cross. Go on, with the hedge on the right, to the end of the field and stop. Fork left off the track and proceed through the middle of the field to cross a footbridge at the corner of a wood. Walk straight ahead through the field to exit onto a track and turn right towards the cottage. In a few paces turn left into a shale track and follow it to the end of the wood on your right. Turn right and maintain direction through three fields to join a lane and turn right for 90 yards (82m). Climb a stile on the right and go forward for 80 yards (73m) and turn left down the centre of the field. At the bottom cross the footbridge

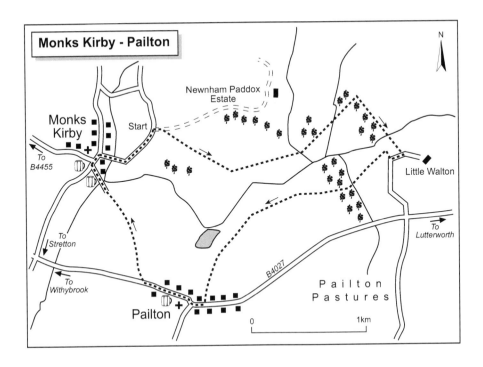

and turn diagonally left to cross the avenue of trees into the next field and go on to a culverted ditch at the end of the second field. Bear right into the next field and cross over a farm road to continue in the same direction to the end of the field and cross a footbridge in the corner.

Climb the steps and turn right for a few paces to reach the edge of a large lake. Turn left and follow the track to a wooden power pole and turn right through a kissing gate into a field. Veer left to another kissing gate in the corner and turn left to exit onto the road in Pailton. Turn right to the road junction and fork right to pass the White Lion on the left. Go on to the working men's club on the right at the edge of the village and turn right into the waymarked bridle path. Follow the path to return to Monks Kirby and pass the Bell Inn to reach the road junction. Turn right and right again to Brockhurst Lane.

Walk 23: Temple Balsall – Oldwich Lane

Temple Balsall is a tranquil corner of England made famous by the crusading Knights Templars and Knights Hospitallers and each year they hold a colourful ceremony in their 13th Century church. Next to the church on Bread Walk stand the almshouses founded in 1677 by Lady Katherine Leveson for ladies of the parish. It is not difficult to picture the ladies in poke bonnet and shawl on their way to church or to collect their bread tokens from the Old Hall. Today men and women dwell here in peaceful retirement.

An easy walk using field paths and a quiet country lane.

Distance: 4 miles (6.5km)
Allow: 2 hours
Map: Ordnance Survey 1:25000 Explorer 221
Grid reference: 208760

How to get there:
From Coventry follow the B4101 through Balsall Common to Temple Balsall and turn left into Fen End Road. Park on the left in the visitor's car park.

The Route:
From the car park cross to the Bread Walk a little to the left and follow it past the almshouses and church to cross a footbridge. In a few paces, where the path divides, turn left through a kissing gate and follow the hedge on the left through a wooden fence to reach a power pole where the path divides again. Turn right and continue along the hedge on the left to exit onto Old Green Lane and turn left for almost one mile (1.6km) passing Sparrow Cock Lane as you go. Just before the junction with Oldwich Lane West turn left over a pair of stiles next to a waymark post and go forward to the far right corner.

Turn right over the footbridge and follow the field edge to a stile in the corner which we ignore. Turn left and follow the hedge on your right to a deep pit surrounded with trees and look for a waymark post on

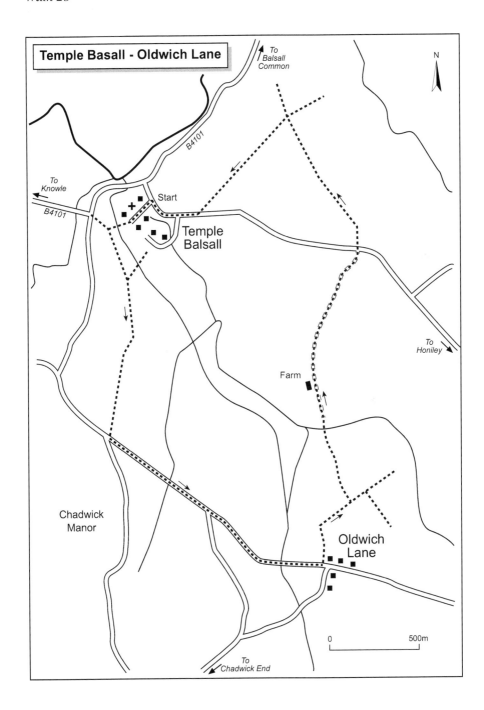

Temple Basall - Oldwich Lane

The Masters House - Temple Balsall

the right. Enter the trail through the bushes and in a few yards/metres exit into a field and follow the short hedge to its end. Go ahead up the centre of the next two fields to a farm on your left and continue along the farm drive to join the road. Cross to an enclosed path a few paces to the right and follow it into a field. Go ahead with the hedge on the right to the end of the third field and ignore the stile in the corner. Turn left on this side of the hedge and follow it to the road. Turn right and in 100 yards (90m) enter the pedestrian route on your right behind the hedge and follow it to the car park.

Walk 24: Stretton on Fosse – Charingworth

The lovely village of Stretton boasts an award winning pub, the Plough Inn which stands opposite the village hall where the walk begins. Beautiful Warwickshire and Gloucestershire scenery unfolds at every turn to make a memorable walk. You will enjoy the quaint little hamlet of Charingworth in the shadow of Goose Hill.

Distance:	4 miles (6.5km)
Allow:	2 hours
Map:	Ordnance Survey 1:25000 OL 45
Grid reference:	220384

How to get there:
From Coventry follow the A423 to Princethorpe and turn right onto the Fosse Way B4455. Continue through Halford for 5 miles (8km) and turn right at the Stretton sign and bear right in the village to pass the church on the left. Go on to the Plough Inn ahead and park at the village hall opposite where the walk begins.

The Route:
Cross the sports field diagonally left from the car park and cross a footbridge in the hedgeline. Turn right to pass through a waymarked field gate and stay in the same direction beneath the power lines. Veer left parallel with the tree line and climb a stile at the end of the field. Go ahead to the next stile in the hedge corner and stay in this direction through the next two fields. Climb a pair of stiles in front, then follow the short hedge on your right to follow the well marked path around Charingworth Grange and turn left down the drive to reach the road. Cross to the path opposite and go forward to the right corner and climb a stile onto the road and turn left.

Continue over Goose Hill to the staggered crossroad in Charingworth and fork left down the descending lane to pass Charingworth Chase Farm on the left. In a further 50 yards (135m) turn left at a footpath sign and go forward between the barn conversions to the tennis court.

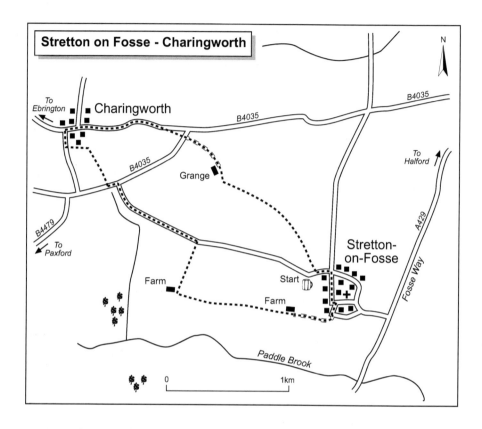

Turn right to cross a stile into a small field and go on through a field gate in the left corner. Turn diagonally left to a field gate when it comes into view about 100 yards (90m) from the corner and exit onto the road. Turn left for 50 yards (45m) and then right into the lane to Stretton and go on for a half mile (800m) to the top of the hill.

Turn right at a footpath sign into a farm drive and follow it to the farm entrance and turn left through a field gate into a bridle path. Go ahead on the left side of the power pole to a bridle gate and continue with the hedge on the left through the fields to return to Stretton. At the road junction turn left and then right down the hill to a crossroads. Turn left to the Plough Inn and the village hall.

Walk 25: Ladbroke – Weddington Hill

This delightful walk is set among a group of gentle hills but our way is flat and easy if you avoid ploughing time. We begin in a beautiful corner of Ladbroke where the 13th century church stands opposite Ladbroke Hall, an unforgettable English scene. The hall is 17th century and was once the home of Lord Rootes, the Coventry car magnate, but is now divided into apartments. The Bell Inn is in the village.

Distance: 3½ miles (5.5km)
Allow: 2 hours
Map: Ordnance Survey 1:25000 Explorer 206
Grid reference: 413588

How to get there:
Follow the A423 from Coventry via the Southam bypass and in one mile (1.6km) turn right at the Ladbroke sign. Bear right along School Lane and Church Road to locate the church where the walk begins. Park in the vicinity with consideration.

The Route:
With your back to the church go forward for 60 yards (55m) to enter a waymarked drive with Ladbroke Hall to your left. Follow it to climb a stile into a field and go ahead to pass through a kissing gate and turn right for 20 yards (18m). Turn left up the field for 80 yards (73m) and fork left to go over the brow of the hill, then descend to a kissing gate at the roadside. Do not exit but turn right in the field on a permissive path to reach a hand gate in 140 yards (130m) and go out to the road. Turn right, using the wider verge opposite, to reach Chapel Ascote Cottages on the right and turn right into the yard. Go ahead through a field gate and exit the paddock in the left corner. Continue straight ahead through the fields for almost one mile (1.6km) to exit over a footplank and fence onto a bridle path. Turn right and stay in this direction to join a single track road and turn right. Go on until the railway bridge comes into view and enter a bridle gate on the right next to the drive to Weddington Farm.

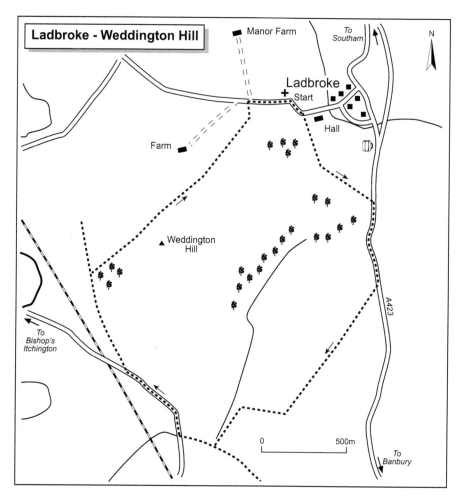

Follow the path into the second field and in 100 yards (90m) turn right at a waymark post and head up the field to the end of the wood on your right. Climb the stile and continue on the other side of the hedge to the end of the second field. Exit through the bridle gate with a farm to your left and go ahead with the church steeple as your guide. Continue through a kissing gate and head for a similar gate in the far left corner. Turn left and go out to the road and turn right to return to the church.

Walk 26: Combrook – Compton Verney

An updated walk to explore the beautiful setting of Combrook and Compton Verney. Capability Brown used the River Dene to create the wonderful lake and near the end of the walk we see the majestic avenue of Wellingtonias, said to be the noblest cedars in England.

Distance:	4 miles (6.5km)
Allow:	2¼ hours
Map:	Ordnance Survey 1:25000 Explorer 206
Grid reference:	307516

How to get there:

Follow the A423 from Coventry to Princethorpe and turn right onto the Fosse Way and continue over the M40 for 5 miles (8km). Turn left into a minor road at the Combrook sign and fork right in the village to park in the vicinity of the church.

The Route:

Walk on for 75 yards (70m) past the church and turn left into a narrow waymarked path, then follow it over a footbridge to reach the end of a cul-de-sac. Turn right into the private garden through the hand gate and turn left through the buildings. Turn right into a green path at the waymark sign and exit over a stile. Turn left through a bridle gate and follow the trail as it curves to the right past the lake to exit into a sheep pasture. Go ahead aiming for a farm and a pair of detached houses and exit at the bridle gate to join the farm road, then follow it to the main road. Turn left and at the top of the hill turn right into a bridle path next to the lodge. Go straight ahead to the farm and turn right to continue into the bridle path and follow it as it curves to the left to reach the road. Turn right to the top of the hill where a footpath crosses the road and turn right through the kissing gate. Go forward through the middle of the field parallel with the hedge on your right to a kissing gate at the end of the field. Continue forward to the Wellingtonias and exit at the kissing gate. Cross the tree lined avenue diagonally left to pick up a woodland trail next to the car park on your

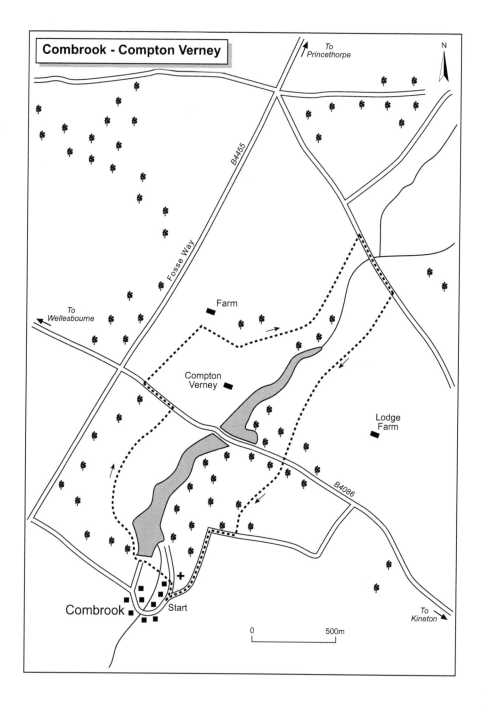

Compton Verney

right, bearing left to a footbridge and go out to the main road. Turn right for 50 yards (45m) and cross carefully to the bus stop and waymark post, then climb the open field diagonally right. Enter the wood at the waymark post and go ahead on the trail to exit into a field. Turn left and climb a stile to join the road, then turn right to return to the church.

Walk 27: Newton Burgoland – Shackerstone

An easy bridle path and the canal guides us to Shackerstone, a mecca for canal boaters and visitors to the Battlefield Line, a tourist railway attraction run by volunteers between Shackerstone and Shenton. There is a pub at each end of the walk.

Distance:	4½ miles (7.25km)
Allow:	2¼ hours
Map:	Ordnance Survey 1:25000 Explorer 232
Grid reference:	364093

How to get there:
From Nuneaton follow the A444 to Twycross and turn right to Snarestone. Follow the signs to Newton Burgoland and just before entering the village look for a small Severn Trent compound on the right next to a bench seat and park in this vicinity.

The Route:
Walk towards the village, forking right into Francis Lane and follow it straight ahead past Corner Farm on the left into a bridle path. Remain in this direction on the bridle path for one mile (1.6km) to reach a single track lane and cross to the stile opposite. Go forward over a stile to join the canal at bridge No. 54 and turn left to follow the water on your right to Shackerstone. Exit at bridge No. 52 and turn right over the bridge, then turn first left into Church Road with the Rising Sun Inn on the left. Continue around the church on the right to reach Congerstone Lane and turn right to pass Station Road on the right. Go on bearing right to cross the canal bridge and then the old railway bridge a few steps ahead.

Turn left to pass the Battlefield Line car park on the left and go on for 180 yards (165m), then turn right into a field at a waymark post. Bear slight left to a stile and go ahead with the hedge on the left to the corner. In the next field follow the hedge on the right to the end of the second field and climb the stile into a short piece of enclosed path.

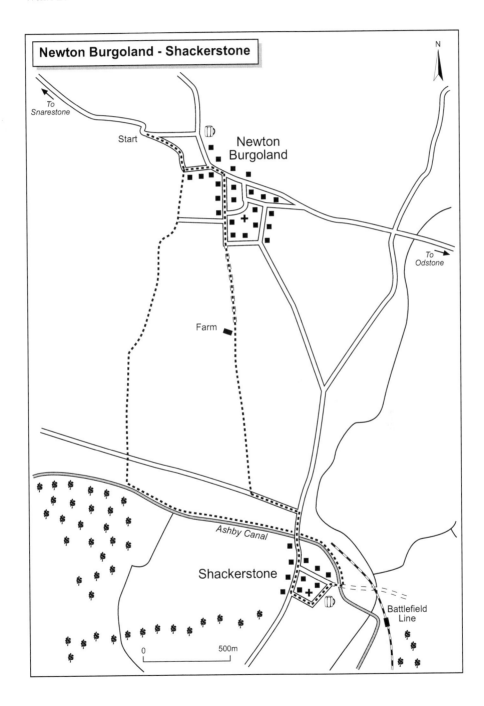

Newton Burgoland - Shackerstone

Exit at a large farmhouse on the left and go forward to the yellow waymark post and stile ahead. Maintain direction along the farm drive and then the lane to return to the village and a T- junction at the main road. Turn left and left again into Francis Lane to return to your car. The Belper Arms Inn is 50 yards (45m) ahead on the main road.

Walk 28:
Around Ettington

This heavily wooded area is ideal for the deer which live here and the sharp eyed walker may see them grazing at the edges of the woods. A lovely walk best enjoyed when the ground is dry due to the sticky nature of the soil.

Distance: 4½ miles (7.25km)
Allow: 2½ hours
Map: Ordnance Survey 1:25000 Explorer 205
Grid reference: 269485

How to get there:
From Coventry follow the A423 to Princethorpe and turn right onto the Fosse Way. Go on to the Ettington crossroads and turn right onto

Ettington Park

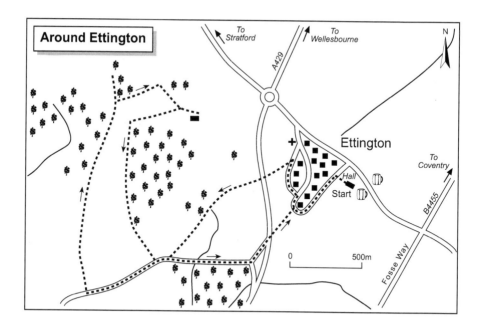

the A422 and pass the White Horse Inn on the left. Turn left into Rogers Lane and park at the community centre on the left.

The Route:
Turn left out of the car park and follow the lane as it doubles back to Rookery Lane and turn left. At the third bend turn left over the stile next to the pony club sign and bear right down the farm track to pass beneath the road bridge. Descend bearing left to a stile next to a field gate and in the next field turn diagonally right to a stile in the corner. Go ahead through the centre of the field and maintain direction over a farm drive to join the road at a stile just to the right of a row of four pine trees and turn right. Walk on for a half mile (800m) to a wood on the left where a bridle path crosses the road and turn right into the track.

Continue to pass through a wood and climb the slope to the corner of another wood on the right. Turn right to follow the wood through a kissing gate and continue to a farm track across your path. Turn right to the farm and just before the barn turn right into the field and head for the far end of the wood on your left. Turn left along the edge of the wood and at the end turn right for 50 yards (45m) and then left along the hedge on the right. At the end of the hedge, go forward to join the road over a stile and turn left. Remain on the road to reach the main road and turn left through the lay-by, crossing with care to the left side of a traffic sign. Enter a trail through the bushes (no waymark post here) and follow it as it becomes a redundant lane and return to the village. Turn right into Rogers Lane and follow it to the car park.

Walk 29: Berkswell – Catchems Corner

A grand walk perhaps for the more adventurous with many stiles and twists and turns but the waymarking is excellent. There may also be a few muddy patches due to the crossing of cattle but nothing too serious for the well shod walker.

Distance: 5 miles (8km)
Allow: 2 hours
Map: Ordnance Survey 1:25000 Explorer 221
Grid reference: 245791

How to get there:
From Hearsall Common in Coventry follow Broad Lane to Berkswell and go over the crossroads to park in the parish car park on the right.

The Route:
Turn right out of the car park and in 70 yards (65m) turn left through a brick arch to enter a field. Go forward to the end of the third field and climb a stile to continue on the other side of the hedge to the end of the field. Turn right for 50 yards (45m) to a stile and head up the field to the farm and follow the farm drive to the road.

Cross to the stile and go down the middle of the field to a footbridge just past the power pole and go on through the middle of the open field to a hedge corner. With the hedge on the left maintain direction through the fields to join the road and cross to a stile on your right and then follow the path to the railway line and turn left.

Go over the railway bridge and climb the stile in front to veer right to a kissing gate on the old railway line. Cross over and descend to a footplank and go ahead through the fields to exit onto the road in the left corner. Turn left into the farm road and follow it until it turns left to the farm and then climb the stile in front. Go ahead through three fields and climb a stile into an enclosed path, then turn left to follow it into a field and walk on to join the road.

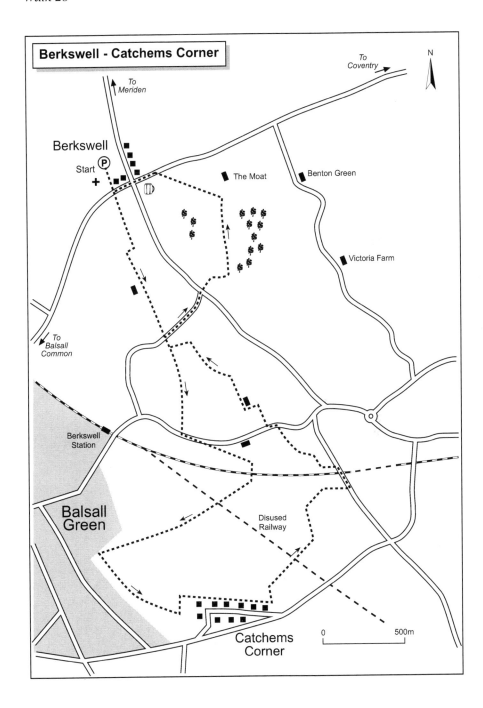

Berkswell - Catchems Corner

To Coventry

N

To Meriden

Berkswell

Start Ⓟ

The Moat

Benton Green

Victoria Farm

To Balsall Common

Berkswell Station

Balsall Green

Disused Railway

Catchems Corner

0   500m

Berkswell

Follow the road ahead to the end and turn left between the last two houses and enter a field. Follow the hedge on the left through the fields to reach the old railway line. Cross over into a field and curve to the left to a stile in the corner and follow the hedge on the left to exit onto the end of a track. Follow the track to a lane and turn right to the main road, then turn left over the railway bridge.

In 60 yards (55m) turn left into a marked drive and go on to a gate across your path, then turn right into a narrow path at a hand gate. Follow the path into a field and go forward to join the road and turn left for 100 yards (90m). Turn right into the drive to Moat House Farm and, where the drive enters two private gardens, climb the stile on the left. Go through the paddock towards the pylon and climb a stile onto a farm road and turn right for 50 yards (45m). Veer left down the open field and at the hedgeline turn left to the bottom of the second field. Turn left for 60 yards (55m) to the footbridge used earlier and retrace your steps back to the road. Turn right and at the end cross into the waymarked drive next to South Lodge and follow it to its end. Turn left over the stile and head through the middle of the field on a well trodden path to exit onto the road in the field corner. Turn left to the crossroads and the car park on the right.

Walk 30: Warwick – Deer Park Wood

An easy walk of two halves with no stiles or ploughed fields and therefore suitable for every season and every ability. The first half borders the old sanatorium at Hatton where the footpaths have sensibly been diverted to the field edges. The second half is a single track lane serving a few farms and cottages and gives a bird's eye view of Warwick and Leamington and beyond.

Distance:	4½ miles (7.25km)
Allow:	2¼ hours
Map:	Ordnance Survey 1:25000 Explorer 221
Grid reference:	265659

How to get there:

From Coventry follow the A46 to exit at the Solihull sign (A4177) and turn left towards Warwick with the cemetery on the left. On the right are Budbrooke Road and Saltisford Canal Trust which can be accessed by turning at the next island. Park at the canal car park and note the closing time on the gate.

The Route:

Return to the road and turn left to carefully cross the island to the traffic lights on the Solihull Road. Cross into the drive to Wedgnock Park Farm and follow it to the farm on your right. Turn left to the corner and turn right to follow the track until it turns left in front of a wood. Turn right and left around the wood and go straight ahead across the next two fields.

At the end turn left towards the houses in Hatton Village and in the corner turn right for a few paces to join another footpath. Head up the slope to pass a bridle path on the left and continue with the hedge on the left through the fields to reach a hedge across your path. Maintain direction on the other side of the hedge to reach the single track lane next to Deer Park Wood and turn right. Remain on the lane for well over one mile (1.6km) to return to Warwick and descend to

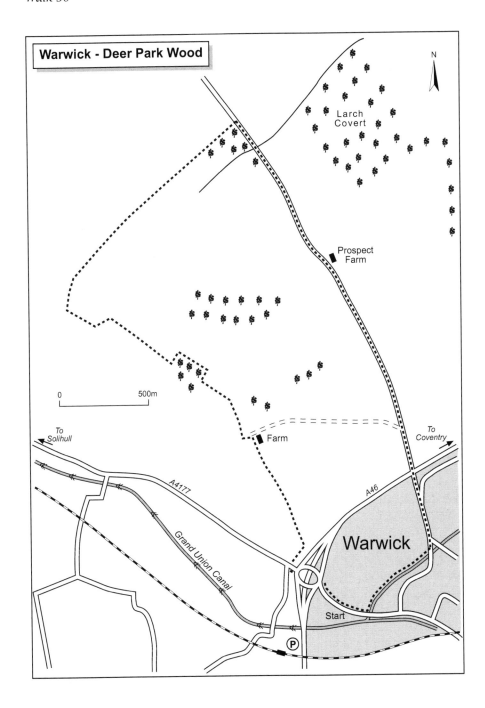

Warwick - Deer Park Wood

Larch Covert

Prospect Farm

N

0   500m

To Solihull

Farm

To Coventry

A4177

A46

Grand Union Canal

Warwick

Start

P

join a main road. Continue past the Volvo centre and turn left into Cape Road to descend the steps onto the canal towpath. Follow the water on your left beneath bridge No. 50 and go on to bridge No. 51 and climb the steps onto the road. Cross with care to Budbrooke Road a little to the left.

Walk 31: Barcheston – Willington

Barcheston found everlasting fame as the birthplace of the Barcheston Tapestries in the mid 16th Century when William Sheldon a wealthy sheep dealer sent his son and a Richard Hyckes to Flanders to learn the art of weaving. They learned well and their tapestries became priceless works of art now residing in galleries and museums. The looms were set up in the shadow of the ancient church and it is fitting that Richard Hyckes rests in the churchyard.

Beautiful countryside unfolds along the way before joining a picturesque lane to Willington and ends with a short stretch along the River Stour.

Distance:	4 miles (6.5km)
Allow:	2 hours
Map:	Ordnance Survey 1:25000 OL 45
Grid reference:	265399

How to get there:
From Coventry follow the A423 to Princethorpe and turn right onto the Fosse Way and continue through Halford. Turn left to Shipston on the A3400 and after the church turn left onto the Brailes road (B4035). Turn first right into a minor road to Barcheston and park in the vicinity of the church.

The Route:
The walk begins at a field gate on the tight bend next to a waymark post. Go forward along the field edge to a footbridge but do not cross. Turn left to reach the road and cross to continue in the same direction to end of the field and climb a stile on your right to proceed on the other side of the hedge to the corner. Turn right and descend to the drive of Hill View Farm and cross into another farm drive through a field gate.

Go on for 170 yards (155m) and veer right through a line of willow trees and head for the stile ahead. In the next field bear diagonally

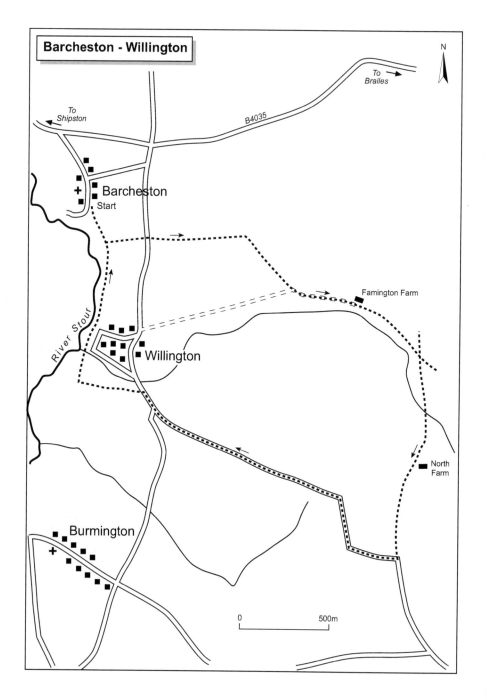

left to a stile between the wooden fence and the start of a hedgeline. Continue in the next field with the hedge on the right to a stile and veer gently right across the open field to cross a footbridge where the path divides. Turn right and stay in this field with the hedge on the right to follow the bridle path past the farm ahead.

Continue along the farm drive to exit onto the road and turn right for a good mile (1.6km) to reach Willington. Turn first left into the village and pass a row of semis to the corner and turn left into an enclosed path and follow it down to the river. Ignore the footbridge and go ahead in the field to a stile and go on, with the river on your left, to return to the footbridge at the start of the walk. Go forward along the field edge to reach your car in the village.

The Crooked Tower - Barcheston

Walk 32: Shuttington – Alvecote Pools

Shuttington is one of Warwickshire's more northerly villages standing on a hill with a tiny ancient church at its highest point. The church once served as a chapel to the ruined Benedictine Priory in the fields below, now surrounded by Alvecote Pools Nature Reserve. The pools were formed by subsidence after the local Alvecote mine closed down and today the scene has returned to nature.

A good walk at any time and the Wulferstan Arms has a garden for the fine days with fine views across the valley.

Distance:	4 miles (6.5km)
Allow:	2 hours
Map:	Ordnance Survey 1:25000 Explorer 232
Grid reference:	256054

How to get there:

From Nuneaton follow the A5 to Grendon and turn right at the island signed for Warton. Go on over a canal bridge to a T-junction and turn left to Polesworth. Turn right over the river bridge and continue to a T-junction and turn left along Linden Lane. At the second turn on the right turn right to Shuttington and pass through the village to its far end where parking may be available at the village hall on the left.

The Route:

Walk back to the village store and turn right into Milner Drive. In the left corner pass through a kissing gate and descend the centre of the field to the next gate. Bear left to a footbridge and cross the next field in the same direction to exit onto the end of a lane at the end of the spinney.

Go ahead over a pair of stiles into a field with a pylon and continue with the lake on the left. Follow the fence to a gated field corner and climb the stile on the left. Stay in the same direction with a fence on the right to reach a culverted brook and stile. Walk on along the field edge to the corner and turn right for 50 yards (45m) to the next corner.

Shuttington

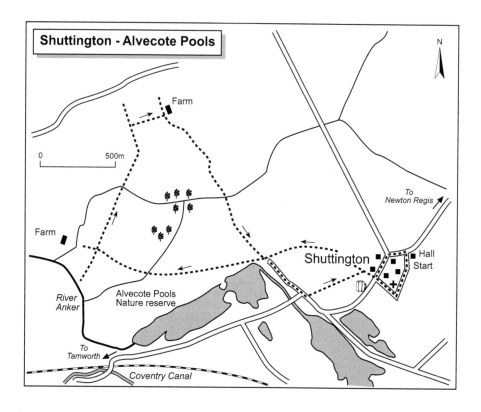

Turn left with the hedge on the left and at the end climb a stile on the left. Turn sharp right to an adjoining stile next to a field gate and follow the concrete path to its end and then the field edge to the wood ahead. Go forward on the farm track until it turns right to the farm and follow it up to the farm drive, then turn right onto the Bridle path.

Stay on the path as it enters an enclosed section between two fields and continue to exit onto the lane at the start of the walk. Turn left and follow the lane to a junction and enter a kissing gate on your left. Bear gently right to a footbridge and gate and continue up the hill to the kissing gate used on the outward journey. Return to the village store and cross into Church Lane and follow the path to the end of the churchyard. Exit into an enclosed path and at the road go forward to join the main road and the village hall is to the right.

Also from Sigma Leisure:

Walks in the Forest of Dean and Wye Valley
Dave Meredith

The Forest of Dean and Wye Valley is a paradise for both the keen rambler and the casual stroller. The 22 walks described in this book are along easy footpaths taking you to spectacular viewpoints, along woodland glades carpeted with bluebells, daffodils and foxgloves, and under the dappled shade of its golden autumn canopy.
£8.99

Walking with Kids
Games and activities to make walking fun
Angela Youngman

Going for a walk can be great fun, educational and healthy. This book offers games and activities introducing kids to the environment whilst walking include tracking, looking for signs of changing seasons, mini beast hunting, feather collecting and art and craft activities in woods, forests, open country, rivers, seaside, towns and evening walks.
£8.99

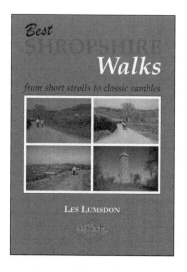

Best Shropshire Walks
from short strolls to classic routes
Les Lumsdon

The walks in this book are located in all parts of the county. Several feature fine hill walking on the Welsh borderlands, including stretches along Offa's Dyke, The Long Mynd and Caer Caradoc. Otheres start from delightful villages and hamlets in the north and east of the county, such as Acton Burnell, Myddle, Stottesdon and Welshampton. Clear maps and a selection of photographs are included.
£8.99

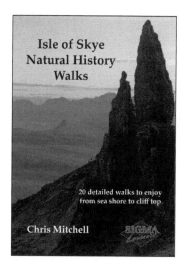

Isle of Skye Natural History Walks
20 detailed walks to enjoy from sea shore to cliff top
Christopher Mitchell

An alternative guide to the wildlife and geology of Skye detailing where to see the island's lesser-known natural history. There are 20 walks based around Portree, Dunvegan, Broadford and Sleat together with detailed maps and quality photographs. Skye has long been regarded as a special place for the birdwatcher, the geologist, the botanist and marine biologist. By taking time to 'stand and stare' you will discover for yourself this hidden side of Skye – one that complements the traditional image of seascapes and mountain views.
£9.99

Walking in the Footsteps of Robin Hood
in Nottinghamshire
Jill Armitage

Walking in the Footsteps of Robin Hood roots out the places mentioned in traditional old tales and visits the locations that Robin and his men would have known. Walk through some of middle England's finest countryside on miles of well-marked footpaths to interesting historical sites associated with the outlaw legend. Stoops, caves, wells and stones with the outlaws names have been traced and woven into the walks taking you through Robin Hood country.
£8.99

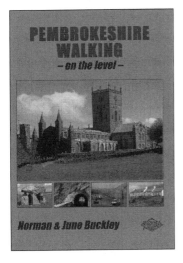

Pembrokeshire Walking
On the level
Norman & June Buckley

This is the sixth volume of the popular and well-establsihed series of 'level walks' books. Discover both the breath-taking splendour of the Pembrokeshire coast and its diverse inland landscape. The 25 comparatively short, easy walks in this book include clear route directions, map and a brief description of features encountered along the way as well as recommendations for refreshment.
£8.99

Walks in the Forest of Dean and Wye Valley
Dave Meredith

The Forest of Dean and Wye Valley is a paradise for both the keen rambler and the casual stroller. The 22 walks described in this book are along easy footpaths taking you to spectacular viewpoints, along woodland glades carpeted with bluebells, daffodils and foxgloves, and under the dappled shade of its golden autumn canopy.
£8.99

Best Tea Shop Walks in the Isle of Wight
Jacqui Leigh

The Isle of Wight is a wonderful place to walk with 500 miles of footpaths, the highest footpath density in the UK, and numerous teashops in beautiful locations. The walks in this book vary in length and difficulty; some include at least part suitable for wheelchair users or pushchairs, giving the option of 'there and back' walks. The teashops range from the very tradition to modern cafe style establishments.
£8.99

All of our books are available through booksellers.
For a free catalogue, please contact:

Sigma Leisure, Stobart House, Pontyclerc
Penybanc Road, Ammanford SA18 3HP

Tel: 01269 593100 Fax: 01269 596116

info@sigmapress.co.uk   www.sigmapress.co.uk